About the National Science and Technology Council

The National Science and Technology Council (NSTC) was established by executive order Nov. 23, 1993. This Cabinet-level Council is the principal means within the executive branch to coordinate science and technology policy across the diverse entities that make up the federal research and development enterprise. Chaired by the President, the NSTC is made up of the Vice President, the Director of the Office of Science and Technology Policy, Cabinet Secretaries and Agency Heads with significant science and technology responsibilities, and other White House officials.

A primary objective of the NSTC is the establishment of clear national goals for federal science and technology investments in a broad array of areas spanning virtually all mission areas of the executive branch. The Council prepares research and development strategies that are coordinated across federal agencies to form investment packages aimed at accomplishing multiple national goals.

The Subcommittee on Biometrics and Identity Management was chartered by the National Science and Technology Council (NSTC) Committee on Technology (COT) and has been in operation since 2003. The purpose of the Subcommittee is to advise and assist the COT, NSTC, and other coordination bodies of the Executive Office of the President on policies, procedures, and plans for federally sponsored biometric and Identity Management (IdM) activities. The Subcommittee facilitates a strong, coordinated effort across federal agencies to identify and address important policy issues, as well as researching, testing, standards, privacy, and outreach needs. The Subcommittee chartered this Task Force to assess the status of and challenges related to IdM technologies and to develop recommendations regarding the federal government's science and technology needs in this area. Additional information about the Subcommittee is available at www.biometrics.gov.

Acknowledgements

The Task Force would like to thank the following individuals for contributing to its success:

- Duane Blackburn (Office of Science and Technology Policy) for his vision to establish the Task Force and to populate it with individuals with such varying foci;
- Jim Dray (National Institute of Standards and Technology) and Judith Spencer (General Services Administration) for effectively managing the Task Force through six months of weekly meetings;
- FBI contractors Michelle Johnson (BRTRC) and Martin Harding (BRTRC) for managing the administrative aspects of the Task Force;
- James Ennis (State), Deborah Gallagher (DHS), William Gravell (DOD), Niels Quist (DOJ), and Bill Brykczynski (STPI) for chairing the Task Force's subordinate working teams;
- William Gravell (DOD) for the innumerable hours he personally devoted to massaging the views of the Task Force members into a cohesive, agreeable description in this report;
- Karen Evans (OMB), Carol Bales (OMB), and the members of the CIO Council, for their assistance in identifying the current status of IdM in the federal government;
- The staff at the Science and Technology Policy Institute (under contract to OSTP), for analyzing data received from the CIO Council;
- The staff at BRTRC, Inc., (under contract to FBI) for editing and graphics support; and
- The IDM Task Force members, who provided input and contributed a significant amount of their time over the course of the six-month effort, are listed in Annex B.

CONTENTS

INDEX OF FIGURES AND TABLES

EXECUTIVE SUMMARY

Introduction

Identity Management (IdM) has existed throughout history to serve both public and private purposes. It has continuously evolved to match changing operational needs, to take advantage of new capabilities, and to stay consistent with the societal conventions of the day. The most recent advancement in IdM has been its transition into the modern digital world, which has provided a wealth of previously impossible capabilities to support both security and convenience needs. Digital IdM systems are becoming increasingly commonplace, and their explosive growth is expected to continue.

> For the purposes of this Task Force, Identity Management means "the combination of technical systems, rules, and procedures that define the ownership, utilization, and safeguarding of personal identity information. The primary goal of the IdM process is to assign attributes to a digital identity and to connect that identity to an individual." The terms of reference for this Task Force are at Annex A.

To date, this growth has been driven by the need to meet independent mission needs (including both screening applications and access control). As these missions continue to expand, overlaps across missions will become more and more pervasive. This is an undeniable truth, as all IdM systems relate back to an individual — actions taken within one system will potentially impact data and/or decisions in other systems. A holistic, cross-mission analysis and planning cycle has not previously been performed, presumably because of the tremendous scope of the task and the duty's inherent social sensitivity. This daunting task was assigned to the National Science and Technology Council's (NSTC) Task Force on Identity Management (Task Force), as a continuation of independently developed and managed government IdM systems will encounter operational, technological, and privacy issues that will become increasingly difficult to manage.

The Task Force's scope was limited to federal government systems, with the full understanding that these systems frequently rely on and impact IdM systems beyond federal control. This report presents an overview of the current state of federal IdM systems and also presents a high-level vision of how these systems can be holistically designed to provide better services while increasing privacy protection. The purpose of this report is to initiate further discussion on this vision, inform policy decisions, and provide direction on which to base near-term research.

Task Force Work

The Task Force was chartered to study federal IdM over a six-month period, with a broad range of representation from different government missions, and was given three primary tasks:

- Provide an assessment of the current state of IdM in the U.S. government;

- Develop a vision for how IdM should operate in the future;

- Develop first-step recommendations on how to advance toward this vision.

The Task Force undertook two overlapping approaches to determine the current state of IdM in the U.S. government, a detailed assessment of publicly available Privacy Impact Assessments and an OMB-issued survey to the Federal Chief Information Officers' Council. The combined analysis showed that there are more than 3,000 systems within the U.S. government that utilize Personally Identifiable Information (PII), and the vast majority of these were designed and are managed independently from one another. These facts contribute to several issues with the current state:

- Duplicative identity data is often stored in multiple locations within the same agency, as well as across agencies, causing a negative impact on accuracy and complicating an individual's attempt at redress;

- A lack of commonly used standards makes appropriate cross-function collaboration difficult, thus impacting both time-sensitive mission needs as well as reducing personal privacy;

- Privacy protection efforts vary in complexity across agencies;

- There is no single government-wide forum responsible for coordinating and homogenizing IdM efforts across the U.S. government.

The IdM Task Force's vision for the future is a substantially more organized Identity Management framework. A fundamental precept for this vision is a realization that not all PII is created equal. Some PII will be useful for broad range of applications, while others are only useful within the context of a specific application and should not be shared outside that application. PII within both of these categories also have varying levels of sensitivity and should be managed accordingly.

The Task Force's vision includes a federated approach for leveraging broad-use PII elements to maximize accuracy, availability, privacy protection, and management of this data. Individual applications would access this data through a network grid, which can be established using common technical standards and policies to ensure appropriate use and control. Once verified, broad-use PII can be augmented with application-specific PII in order to make operational decisions. To this end, we make the following assumptions:

- Identity and the management of all the personal identifiable qualities of identity information are considered a critical asset in sustaining our security posture;

- To the extent available and practicable, a very high confidence in an asserted identity is recommended as the basis for authorization for access to government applications regardless of assurance level required. For example, Personal Identity Verification (PIV) credentials required by HSPD-12 and used by federal employees and contractors are available and provide for a very high level of confidence and could be used for accessing all applications — even those requiring lower levels of assurance;

- There is an expectation that revocation of identity data and the related authorizations are executed in accordance with government-wide standards throughout all applications (whether used to support logical or physical access);

- There is an understanding that management and protection of identity is not the responsibility of any one or a few federal agencies, but rather the responsibility of all federal agencies to enable. Identity is a component of each and every transaction. If one federal agency fails to carry out their responsibility, access to our networks and facilities will be significantly jeopardized.

Several top-level goals and characteristics for the government's proposed state of IdM can thus be described as:

- Configuration and operation of a "network of networks" to securely manage digital identities, based on a set of common data elements for stored PII that will allow it to be leveraged by a broad range of applications;

- Security of process, data transmission, and storage; this includes and embraces all features of confidentiality, integrity, authenticity, and privacy, including use of encryption and multifactor authentication;

- Auditability of processes, with complete, automatic, and secure record keeping;

- Ubiquitous availability, at global distances, of strong verification of stored digital identity when called for or needed to support an authorized application;

- Standards-based connectivity, interoperability, and extensibility of supporting IT architecture;

- Preservation of application-specific PII data under control of application sponsors, with minimal exposure to unauthorized access or unnecessary transmission across networks;

- Ability of prospective application sponsors to develop, install, and operate applications in a way that permits the supporting IT grid to be seen as a freely available, ubiquitous service.

The above elements form the tenets of a strategy to manage and protect identity within all federal agencies. Anticipated benefits over the current state include:

- Enhanced accuracy and management of PII that is used by multiple applications;

- Clear separation of application-specific PII and tighter controls to ensure this information isn't shared across domains;

- A uniform, more transparent approach of handling PII;

- Minimization of duplicative efforts to generate, maintain, and safeguard PII;

- Providing the government a better understanding of and ability to macro-manage its IdM activities.

This report offers a set of recommendations (see Section 4) organized into specific subject areas as follows:

- Standards and Guidance;

- Architecture;

- Science and Technology Considerations;

- Government-wide Coordination.

The Science and Technology recommendations may be acted upon immediately, as the success of those efforts will impact further analyses and policymaking required to provide depth and direction to the Task Force's initial vision.

Toward that end, the Task Force recommends an enduring IdM forum to visualize and address IdManagement issues holistically, in policy and technology. This process should seek to frame the governmental agenda in this broad area, inform the standards and guidance development activities, and guide the further refinement of the IdM architecture. In so doing, it should guide activities that will expand and refine our total understanding and support the development of consensus within an informed public regarding the whole range of IdManagement issues and opportunities within the federal enterprise.

Conclusion

It is important to note that the Task Force does not see this report as being the "final" analysis of the IdM needs of the federal government, nor is it considered to be a comprehensive treatment of the subject in a level of detail sufficient to determine formal policy. Rather, it is an initial study that provides a common foundation and vision on which to base future research, discussions, studies, and, eventually, policymaking. The Task Force aimed to make this report as intellectually comprehensive as possible within available time and resources, seeking, above all, to recognize and treat IdM in its full dimensions, including its growing importance to the conduct of government.

In contemplating the current state of IdM in the federal government, and thinking about the future direction, one may paraphrase Winston Churchill:

"It is not the end, nor even the beginning of the end; but it is, perhaps, the end of the beginning..."

1 INTRODUCTION

Identity Management (IdM) is a topic that has grown rapidly and adapted significantly in recent years. Although the underlying processes have been in use for centuries, the term itself is a relatively recent invention, created in response to the need to collectively address issues encompassing related areas of technology, policy, and process. Components of IdM systems include biometrics, identity cards, and user ID/passwords/personal identification numbers (PIN) to support access control (both physical and logical) and supporting information technology (IT) architectures. To all of this must be added a wealth of law, regulation, policy, and, above all, awareness of and sensitivity to the attitudes and views of the organizations — including society itself — within which such systems are proposed to be installed and operated. Within the latter, preservation of rights and privileges and protection of privacy are of foremost importance.

The underlying function of identification has been a part of the human experience since the growth of social complexity introduced differentiated roles, rights, privileges, and resources into communities. Some of these "unique abilities" came with membership of a class or group, while others represented individual characteristics. Sometimes there was an identifying badge, mark, object, or other way to visually distinguish the individual with a specific role; sometimes this could only be known from personal interaction.

In modern times, society has developed systems to characterize individuals for purposes of establishing their authorizations (e.g., driver's license), support security needs (e.g., fingerprint matching as an aspect of criminal investigation), or to streamline delivery of specific services or entitlements (e.g., Social Security number). In the absence of a purpose-built IdM framework, these have sometimes been used as *de facto* "ID systems," with uneven results.

Even more recently, the advent of the digital age has seen the explosive proliferation of citizen-level ability to access information and resources globally via the Internet. As the Internet became a preferred mechanism for many individuals to receive information, communicate, and conduct business, official organizations responded. In the name of customer convenience, they began to design computer network-accessible tools and resources to perform functions once only achievable through in-person interaction with government officials in their offices. The proliferation of these online services exploded and continues to do so today.

The response to the terrorism acts of 9/11 and other events has made security screening part of many processes and activities; the ability to conduct such screening effectively relies heavily on the availability of standard and secure identity documentation. The enormous proliferation of the number, nature, location, and frequency of such checks poses a challenge in itself, regarding the design of scalable and accurate systems to support screening needs.

Individuals became victims of "identity theft" and frauds of many types, since they were now dealing with resources worth trying to steal. Federal organizations, increasingly dependent on networked online resources and tools to conduct the business of government, became concerned about the vulnerability of these systems to cyber attack, and the increasingly-serious consequences if such attacks could be conducted successfully. Over time, these "negative motivators" have become matters of increasing concern.

At the same time, however, the development of better and more widely accessible capabilities to access information and do useful work made the online domain more attractive as a place to conduct serious business. This included support to processes in ways that had never been possible before. The "upside potential" of safe and secure transactions, continuously accessible at any distance, began to take substance.

In so doing, the importance of establishing one's identity to support these interactions became increasingly important. At this point, the casual manner of "identification" employed up until that time often became insufficient to establish the trusted relationship required for these transactions. Beyond these considerations related to individuals who are "U.S. persons and others known as friendly," the federal government's total IdM must also include the ability to detect and re-detect (if previously having been ascertained to represent a threat) persons who place American citizens or facilities at risk. The identification data related to these may be tenuous, ambiguous, incomplete, and may not conform to any specific technical formats or standards. A major function of the total IdM system is to facilitate the development of speedy and accurate judgments regarding such threats, using all available and relevant information.

Finally, there are persons who are "unknown" in terms of their security risk, in that they have neither been vetted through governmental processes to establish in their trust identity assertions (e.g., HSPD-12/FIPS-201 standards) nor demonstrated any hostile intent or actions. Data regarding these persons are now being collected under the authority of various programs associated with border controls or foreign national security operations. These people are considered "unknowns," for our purposes.

These various needs for security, privacy, access, service, and the ability to take advantage of emergent capabilities all come together in the modern concept of IdM.

IdM is now beginning to emerge in ways appropriate to its potential. That potential includes the achievement of valuable benefits and new capabilities with improvements that can be measured in several ways. At the same time, IdM will *enhance* personal freedoms, privacy, and self-determination, relative to the status quo, for the conduct of such matters.

This Task Force's purpose is to better understand and report on the potential that IdM offers to improve performance of the full range of government functions, and to seek understanding of the transformation in these matters that modern global telecommunications connectivity has precipitated. From this, the Task Force's recommendations will seek to identify investment and policy priorities that will wisely guide the government forward in this area.

1.1 PURPOSE

The purpose of this report is to:

- Inform policy makers and the public regarding the issues and opportunities associated with IdM;

- Homogenize the IdM discussion within and across government, by seeking to establish common terms, goals, and standards for the whole subject area;

- Provide a vision of the future application and use of IdM in the federal government, for future consideration by agencies, subsequent studies, and policymaking bodies;

- Demonstrate that privacy may be *improved* relative to the status quo, while transitioning identity-related activities into rigorous and accountable IT-based applications;

- Develop, identify, and list some of the most immediate needs in research and development, standards development, technical policy, and technology architecture, as needed to achieve these outcomes. Advancing science and technology in this way will enable agencies to:

  o *Improve the performance of existing* systems and processes, as now fielded, in ways involving minimal time, effort, and expense;

  o *Modify existing* systems to enhance functionality and scalability;

  o *And devise new approaches* to extend usable and responsive IdM service to the whole set of users and their identity assurance needs.

1.2 BACKGROUND AND TASK FORCE CHARTER

Over time, persons and organizations have sought to design means to identify individuals for a broad range of purposes.

The techniques and technologies that have supported these efforts have varied widely and continue to do so today. The general trend has been for these mechanisms to become more rigorous and complex over time as technology has advanced. At the same time, there remains a general understanding that the same level of confidence is not needed for every identity assurance activity and application. Through all of this, there have been several basic premises:

- Regardless of the method used by individuals in remote settings to assert their identity (and, thus, rights or privilege of every sort) to an application or access control system, some knowledge of the granting and status of these privileges was maintained in a separate and distinct location, often by the granting authority;

- If and when changing circumstances altered the privileges of the remote user previously authorized for such purposes, changes only took effect when they could be authoritatively communicated to the remote application or access control system by the granting authority;

- As such, if some emergent problem associated with a user demanded action in less time than it took the real authority to respond, then local initiative was necessary; this approach sometimes worked but opened the way to abuse and excess;

- These systems — a defined set of roles and privileges, linked to a granting and controlling authority who maintained some kind of records about the process — tended to proliferate. The extent and nature of the data required to support these systems was generally unique; this led to the creation of redundant, parallel "stovepipes," or, in some cases, communications channels between the granting authority and the remote activity.

And so the IdM process has remained until very recently, by and large, a process where:

- Information is collected and stored to establish eligibility, entitlement, or to confer authority on persons who are to be embraced within a *specific* IdM system;

- Those persons are empowered in various ways by the authority controlling the role or privilege involved; they are often provided with some physical token of that role to aid them in asserting the granted privilege when at a distance from the actual authority.

- As the authority manages the process, he/she may add, delete, or alter persons or authorities to the system;

- Such changes take effect with variable ease, speed, and confidence, depending on the connection between the authority and the population embraced within the system;

- All of this is done largely in parallel, by various subject-matter-specific IdM systems, with the cost and effort of collecting and managing all information and transactions replicated in each one. The result is similar to the situation depicted in Figure 1.

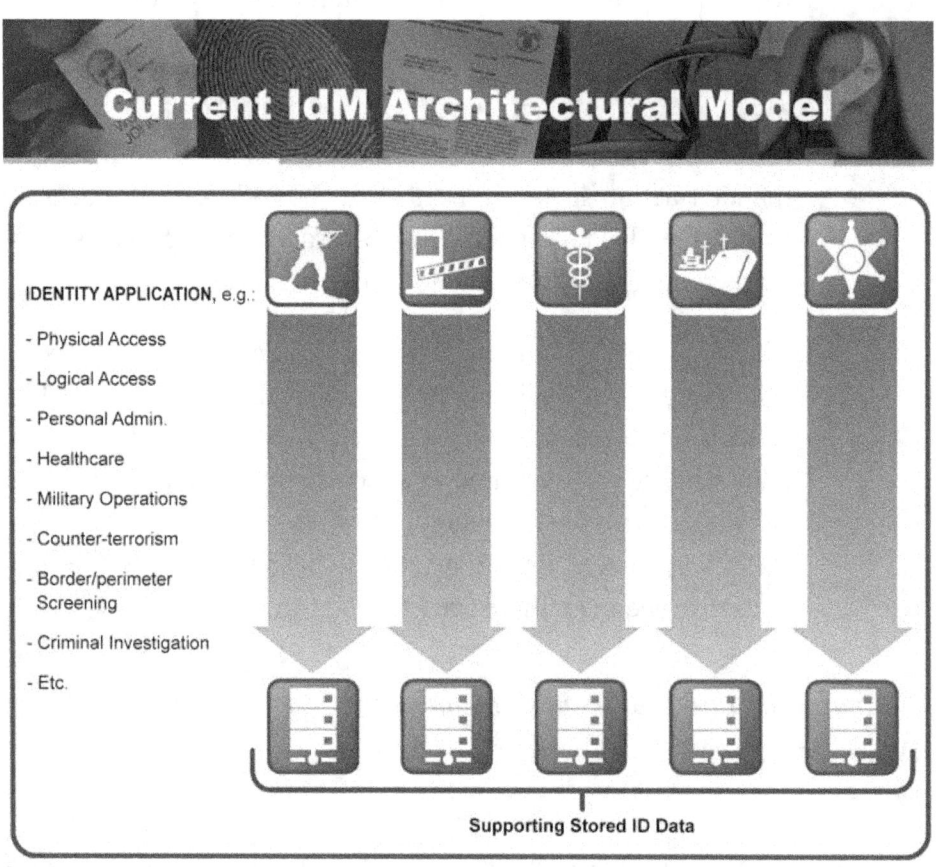

Figure 1. Current IdM Architectural Model

As noted, one aspect of IdM relates to **_security screening_** processes of one sort or another, however, there is another, widely used aspect of IdM that is concerned with establishing identity in order to conduct business. The true value of an IdM system is realized when it is used to empower service providers, such as the federal government, to flexibly control access to applications and information, empowering the network grid to support persons in the conduct of their professional and personal business, and apply resources to uses of their choosing. These *value-added applications* of IdM offer measurable savings in time and money.[1] f designed wisely, these allow individuals to largely control the nature and extent of their own participation in identity assurance processes. To some extent, this can be based on voluntary enrollment on the basis of value recognizable to them personally.

Most recently, advancements in IT plus evolution in the nature of and increasing need for security screening have led the federal government to develop a number of ID-related programs for specific applications and groups of people. These programs have driven recognition that relates to the historic approaches outlined above. IdM in America today must be:

- Adaptive, responsive, and universally accessible;

- Attuned to social acceptability and privacy, so as to be embraced and genuinely valued by its users;

- Extensible in scale (numbers) and scope (different types of activities it can embrace), due to explosively growing need and interest, even by many who may lack deep technical training or experience;

- Easy to use and maintain, for the same reasons;

Secure and effective, leaving minimal risk of exploitation, alteration, or misuse at any level of the system, and allowing all parties to be confident of its use.IdM in America today can be:

- All but invisible to the end-user, even while being ubiquitously available; Of genuine, measurable value to individual users and "application-sponsoring" organizations and authorities (those

---

[1] See OMB Memorandum M-06-22, "*Cost Savings Achieved Through E-Government and Line of Business Initiatives.*"

whose roles and powers allow or compel them to organize the performance of some identity-based activity);

- More responsive to law, policy, and social sensitivities as regards privacy than has often historically been the case with similar activities;

- Of streamlined/simplified structure from the point of view of individuals and sponsors, allowing the design, development, and management of standards-compliant applications at lower cost and with more local control and initiative;

- Designed to provide convenience and efficiency by allowing secure reuse of credentials in multiple applications.

CHARTER:

It is toward these ends that the work of this Task Force was initiated, as chartered by the Executive Office of the President (EOP), National Science and Technology Council (NSTC), and Subcommittee on Biometrics and Identity Management.

The NSTC Subcommittee on Biometrics and Identity Management has been coordinating interagency biometric efforts since 2002. Initial activities focused on rapid advancement of the technology, developing standards at the national and international level, advancing and performing evaluations, and promoting privacy protection. As the technology advanced, so, too, did its usage by government agencies to solve important operational missions. In 2006, the Subcommittee initiated activities to improve coordination of these operational systems and to jointly determine several issues that would serve as a common foundation for agencies as they began development of their next generation systems. It quickly became clear that the need for coordination was expanding beyond biometrics to higher-level Identity Management (IdM) issues. Once briefed on this conclusion, the NSTC Committee on Technology readily agreed and expanded the scope of the then biometrics-focused Subcommittee to also coordinate identity management S&T issues. Concurrently with these discussions, a Defense Science Board Task Force was also studying how to improve coordination within the Department of Defense.[2] It, too, reached the conclusion that successful biometrics coordination will require, by default, coordination on broader identity management issues.

In addition to leading NSTC activities, EOP personnel have other responsibilities, such as reviewing and approving agency rulemaking documents and Congressional testimony, participating in policy coordination committees and other bodies (such as the Identity Theft Task Force and the Chief Information Officer (CIO) Council), and representing the U.S. in international technology and privacy discussions. The unique across-the-government insight afforded by these tasks made it clear that there was overlap among government programs in IdM technology and policy issues, duplication of efforts to overcome those issues, and gaps in required coordination to enable these systems to achieve maximum efficiency and privacy protection.

In the summer of 2007, OSTP hosted a small series of meetings amongst offices within the EOP to discuss IdManagement issues. After some initial analysis, the group agreed that a more detailed analysis approach was required. As a result, OSTP, in consultation with other EOP bodies, agreed to assign this task to the Subcommittee.

The Subcommittee thus formally established the NSTC Task Force on Identity Management to assess the status of and challenges related to IdM technologies and develop recommendations regarding federal government's science and technology needs in this area. For the purposes of this Task Force, Identity Management means, "The combination of technical systems, rules and procedures that define the ownership, utilization, and safeguard of personal identity information. The primary goal of the Identity Management process is to assign attributes

---

[2] Report of the Defense Science Board Task Force on Defense Biometrics, *Office of the Under Secretary of Defense for Acquisition, Technology and Logistics,* 2007 http://www.acq.osd mil/dsb/reports/2007-03-Biometrics.pdf.

to a digital identity and to connect that identity to an individual." The terms of reference for this Task Force are in Annex A.

1.3 SCOPE

This report addresses the use of IdM within the following scope:

- **Internal to the federal government** to aid in the performance of the full range of tasks and missions requiring internal coordination;

- **Between the federal government and other governmental jurisdictions** (state, local, and tribal);

- **Between the federal government and the international community**;

- **Between the federal government and U.S. organizations, commercial entities, and individuals accessing government resources (both facilities and systems).**

NOTE: What is not addressed in this report is the conduct of personal and/or business matters between and among citizens and commercial enterprises, where the U.S. federal government is not a direct party. This study does not address those issues, and this report makes no recommendations in that regard.

1.4 STATEMENT OF THE PROBLEM

Less than a decade ago, most government IT systems were "stovepipes," legacy systems developed for a specific purpose that did not interoperate with other systems or organizations many remain so today. Advances in modern IT have made interconnection practical, while the changing operational environment makes expanded interoperability necessary, both from the standpoint of practicality and the need to achieve economies of scale through consolidation and streamlining. This has resulted in major improvements in functionality, as seen by an expanded set of end-users. Today it takes seconds to find out the operating hours of government offices online, a job that would have previously required a physical trip, or at least a telephone call. Over the next decade, these same systems will transition to increasingly complex and robust digital architecture and will very likely offer more attractive features at the same time. The government must seek to understand the initiative space available to enhance the performance of its diverse roles and missions. This will permit government to be as consistent as possible with the feel of other network-related relationships available to businesses and citizens.

1.5 THE CASE FOR ACTION

There are both deficiencies and opportunities associated with IdM as currently practiced. These include:

1.5.1 Current Deficiencies

- Cross-organizational coordination. Information and technical capabilities needed for successful performance of complex tasks are distributed geographically and in terms of storage location within data networks.[3] They may also be under control of different organizations, which may employ different data management systems.

- Disparate security management protocols. Federal employees manage numerous credentials (identity cards, user ID/passwords/PINs, etc.) for numerous unique and independent systems. As security concerns have become greater, required periodic password changes and complexity of password construction have all become more stringent, exacerbating challenges to memorization and management.

- Inconsistent Agency Implementation. These make the emergence of a cross-domain trust model difficult. Specific guidance has been

---

[3] It is important to note that the advocated solution is not the centralization of databases. Rather, there is a need to find ways to enable these disparate systems to interoperate.

provided on identity assurance trust levels[4] and minimum technical solutions applicable to each of these levels.[5] However, the full implementation of the guidance by agencies has not yet been fully realized.

- Screening Information Sharing. Many screening systems are used in security operations to establish the risk posed by individuals in various contexts, such as granting visas to enter the United States or allowing access to federal government facilities. Information relevant to these purposes exists in various databases held by various organizations of the federal government. Greater efficiencies can be gained by ensuring individual organizations can better leverage information across multiple identity screening databases to make accurate assessments.

- Inconsistent system-security usages, operating rules and procedures. These permit the introduction of vulnerabilities into systems, based on the existence of these deficiencies in systems to which one is connected. These "vulnerability by association" risks invalidating efforts and expenses associated with systems security.

- Evolving nature of global IT grid demands recognition to preserve capability and system-wide security. The total number of terminal IT devices is increasing exponentially. At the same time, the percentage of systems that are nomadic in their missions and wireless or dynamic in their physical location is also increasing. Finally, there are clear trends in the performance of retail, financial, information, and other commercial processes that move performance away from physical hubs toward remote, but Web-accessible venues. The government is engaged in all of these activities and is affected by these trends. To the extent that these evolving IT architectures represent changes in the security system, these must be accounted for.

---

[4] OMB Memorandum 04-04, *E-Authentication for Federal Agencies.*

[5] NIST SP 800-63, *Electronic Authentication Guidelines.*

- Exploitation of identity information. If users can be deceived into entering their PII on fraudulent sites disguised as real applications, the identity thief is then able to impersonate the user to enter a real application and access all information and resources as if he or she were the genuinely authorized user.

- Interoperability shortfalls. Global interoperability will be achieved by developing a bridging function that enables disparate IdM systems and federations of systems to exchange identity information and reuse existing credentials. This bridging function will permit individual organizations to verify identity claims by querying the data-stores held by others. Some of the major challenges associated with developing standards for the bridging function of an IdM framework are listed below.

  - Discovery and domain resolution. Discovery is the process by which an identity provider can locate the relevant and authoritative identity data, which may be highly distributed and located in different security domains.

  - Need for greater trust. Development of trust involves authentication by each of the parties from a transaction to the level of assurance required by the other party in order to proceed with a transaction. Today, there are no globally agreed technical definitions for levels of trust, nor are there agreed-upon standards to measure levels of trust (i.e., metrics).

  - IdM systems that rely on loosely-coupled identities. When organizations today collaborate with each other, they typically use traditional identity systems in which the identifiers are closely linked to the entity being identified. These may require every organization to have a local account for a user, regardless of justification. This collaboration, especially when it is between changing sets of partners with nomadic user populations, has a number of deficiencies.

  - Lack of consistent metrics. Governmental IdM systems are not currently required to ascertain standard Measures of Performance (MOP) such as Probability of False Acceptance (PFA), where a person is able to falsely claim the identity of another, and Probability of False Rejection (PFR), where a person is unable to claim his/her correct identity. These and similar measures would permit more nearly direct comparison of the performance of specific systems versus each other, and/or accepted standards.

1.5.2 Opportunities

This is where the full value of IdM may be realized. If approached systematically, it is often possible to measure the positive benefits of IdM in tangible and even monetary terms, and thereby support investment in specific capabilities that meet return-on-investment standards to justify the effort. Examples include:

- <u>Ability to capitalize on existing investment in digital ID infrastructure.</u> By Presidential directive,[6] the federal government has established procedures for the basic identification of all federal employees on a common technical standard, called Federal Information Processing Standard (FIPS)-201.[7] This provides for the identification of government personnel on a common, interoperable, and rigorous basis, and the issuance of a standardized credential attesting to that identification. However, this is a developing program which has yet to realize its full potential. While the identity card itself is gaining broad distribution, the extension of this effort and investment into application is currently limited, and existing IT architectures do not always support it. This issue will be addressed in detail below. The ability to develop applications that draw on the capabilities of the FIPS 201 credential to support the whole range of identity assurance activities, at much-improved levels of security and trust relative to identity approaches in com-

---

[6] Homeland Security Presidential Directive 12 (HSPD-12), Policy for a Common Identification Standard for Federal Employees and Contractors, 2004.
http://www.whitehouse.gov/news/releases/2004/08/20040827-8 html.

[7] http://csrc nist.gov/publications/fips

mon use elsewhere, represents a great opportunity for the federal government.

- <u>Ability to achieve efficiencies in design and use of IT architectures.</u> Heretofore, IdM systems have been authorized, designed, and fielded to serve specific purposes. In many cases, the identity-related data used by applications within the IdM systems are the same, but due to lack of good architectural design for information sharing, the data is often duplicated by the individual applications as considered necessary to support their particular needs. This leads to a failure to recognize and update basic information in an equal way, wherever located, which in turn gives rise to confusion, delay, and error in practice.

- <u>Ability to rationalize and harmonize data management standards and policies across historically separate architectures.</u> Interoperability has components of technology and policy. By seeing the total federal IdM activity holistically, common standards and practices will not only enhance performance, but also provide more auditable visibility into use of personal information of a private nature.

- <u>Ability to achieve efficiencies associated with single sign-on to access multiple systems</u>. The average federal employee, in any agency, uses numerous IT systems for various professional and administrative purposes. In almost every case, these are unique, stand-alone designs that require their own card, key, user ID/password, or other form of log-on. They also demand different levels of trust, based on the sensitivity of the application. single IT system sign-on at a high level of trust leveraging PIV credentials could permit federal employees to establish their identity at one system or portal and then access a wide range of applications, as required to perform their work and consistent with their privileges.

1.6 INTRODUCTION TO KEY TERMS AND CONCEPTS

As discussed above, IdM is a set of goals and concepts currently implemented in a broad and diverse mass of technology. The complexity of the current legacy architectures and systems makes any simple description of the federal-scope IdM system elusive and necessarily incomplete. This is complicated by the fact that in many cases, different terms are used to describe essentially the same processes. This report will use several terms that may not be in common use today. In the interest of ease of reader understanding, some of the most important ones are listed here, as they will be used throughout the report. A full glossary may be found at Annex K.

Personally Identifiable Information — The foundational issue in approaching any IdM system is personal information — how it is collected, stored, shared, and used. The term most often applied to these data is "personally identifiable information" (PII). Generally, PII is defined as "[t]he information pertaining to any person which makes it possible to identify such individual (including the information capable of identifying a person when combined with other information even if the information does not clearly identify the person)." This may be interpreted as "any information which identifies a person to any degree."

The Task Force holds that "PII" occupies a continuum of sensitivity and that it assumes a different character depending on the place it is used in the IdM system. These concepts will be explained in greater detail in section 2.4.1. Later sections of the report will introduce structural components of the overall federal IdM system, with descriptions and relevant terms.

Sponsor — An authority, whether based in law, policy, or organizational/personal initiative, who seeks to organize identification information to regulate the conduct of some task or activity, where not all persons have identical rights or privileges to perform that activity.

Applications — The ability to collect or use identity and other data in a specific context. Sponsors manage the access to applications, in the form of privileges available to "identifiable" persons by entitlement or enrollment. Applications manage and store transaction and other specific data as generated by an individual in their interaction within the application.

Enrollees — The persons for whom digital identities have been created and stored within an IdM system.

Beyond these, any given ID system *may* include identity cards, biometrics, user ID/passwords/PINs, and other unique features. Ideally, these are selected and used as indicated by the scope, scale, and nature of the need and use, since these features are not equally attractive in every ID situation.

This report seeks to develop an understanding of an *objective ID architecture with three primary components:*

- Digital Identity Repositories;
- Privilege Applications;
- The Global Telecommunications Grid.

Each of these will be discussed at length below. When these elements are assembled into a system, they may be thought of as relating to each other as shown in Figure 2 below. This simplistic model will be developed in greater detail later in the report, but for now it serves to identify and grossly organize the major IdM system components.

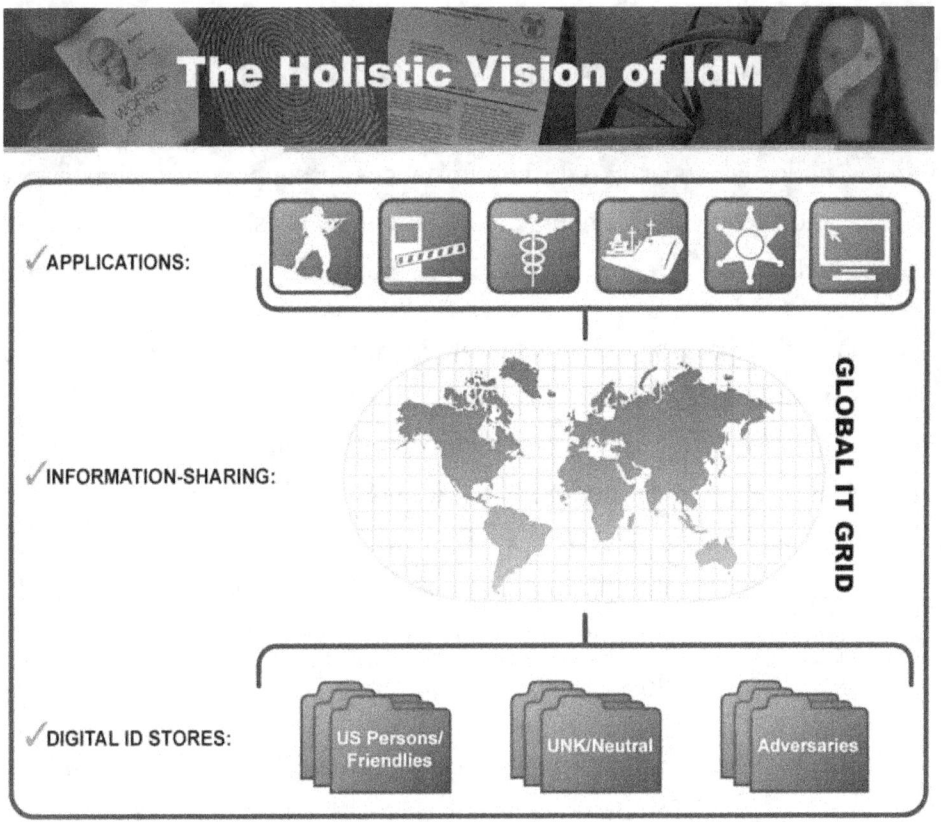

Figure 2. Holistic Vision of IdM

Following is a description of each of these three components of an objective identity architecture:

Digital Identity Repositories — These are the various places where PII is stored. The data in these repositories relate to individuals in three major categories — Friendlies (which encompasses U.S. persons), Adversaries (those known to be hostile to the U.S.), and Unknown.

Friendly individuals are those for whom information has been collected in order to facilitate interaction. Within the federal government scope, these may have been collected and stored voluntarily for a number of systems that perform services to various groups (Social Security services, education loans, etc.).

Alternatively, "adversary" data represents information gathered in the conduct of military or intelligence operations overseas.

Finally, there are "the unknowns" — persons who are not registered in one of the federal government systems in either of the ways discussed above, but are not known to be hostile to U.S. interests. Data on individuals in this category are now being collected under certain circumstances in support of national security operations and are retained under certain circumstances to aid in coordination with allies and identification of adversaries in the future.

Today, these repositories containing identity data associated with the three categories described above exist in many different formats, data standards, and under multiple authorities. They each retain "digital identities" in some form. The security of the identity data these repositories contain, in terms of the information assurance technologies and practices under which they are maintained, is currently uneven. It may also be stated that the confidence and trust of these digital IDs is uneven, based on many factors related to circumstances of collection, technologies, techniques employed, etc.

Privilege Applications — As noted, a "privilege" is a grant of permission to carry out a particular act. In this context, an application is a place where a digital identity to which a privilege has been attached can achieve some outcome involving entitlement to a resource, information, or access. For the most part the exercise of privilege is confined to individuals in the "friendly" category. However, it is equally important to ensure that individuals in the "unknown" or "adversary" categories are not mistakenly granted privileges reserved for "friendly" persons. The small pictures at the application layer of Figure 2 suggest just a few of the myriad potential functions involving identity assurance that may be embraced within such a system, with more being added all the time. As the diagram suggests, these applications may be as diverse as physical access to some location, the ability to access files within an information network, or to support medical or military operations. In fact, the number and range of ID applications is bounded only by the perceived need and imagination of sponsors who seek to perform their missions with efficiency and security.

PII is contained inside both the digital IDs and the privilege applications. However, to optimize protections of privacy, the treatment of these data should differ in both concept and practice, as discussed in detail in section 2.4.1.

<u>Global Telecommunications Grid</u> — The servicing IT grid is critical in achieving access, anywhere in the world, with continuously-available and interoperable systems and data formats, all necessary to support the full range of U.S. government missions. These include screening functions, wherein the objective is to determine what is known about a certain person, in which pursuit applications may request access to multiple other data stores; and access controls, which have the goal of facilitating access to both physical and online resources, by persons to whom such privileges have been granted (i.e. friendly individuals).

Security and privacy of transactions are of paramount importance. To achieve these, privacy is added to classic information assurance features of data confidentiality, authenticity, non-repudiation, and integrity as pursued within government networks.

The next sections will examine each of these foundational elements, both as they exist and are used in current systems (Section 2, The Current State) and in the objective state (Section 3, The Proposed Framework).

2 THE CURRENT STATE

2.1 CURRENT FEDERAL IDM SYSTEM COMPONENTS

2.1.1 Digital ID Stores

IdM tends to be approached with targeted solutions to meet specific and internally-defined agency needs. While this strategy may be effective at solving narrowly scoped problems, it has led to the growth of "stovepiped" legacy systems in complex and non-interoperable configurations. These patchwork architectures inhibit cooperation and hinder the efficient delivery of government services across the spectrum of stakeholders. To a certain extent, this situation arises from some of the essential characteristics of government as an organization. It is natural for applications and information stores to become isolated in an environment where:

- Innovation and change may be valued less than stability, continuity, and predictability;
- Inter-departmental boundaries are fixed and stakeholder boundary crossing is discouraged;
- Policy changes may drive systems redesign or reconfigure their uses;
- Agency initiatives may conflict or overlap; and
- The scope of activities can be expansive and at times unrealistic.[8]

This is the current situation in IdM, which leads to duplicative identity data often being stored in multiple locations within the same agency, e.g., once for

---

[8] Sundberg & Sandberg, 2006

human resources and once for the employee phone directory. The data may also be duplicated for procedural reasons. For example, different operating divisions within the same agency will often not share identity information about transferred employees due to questions over whose budget will be charged for collecting and managing the data. This results in both divisions collecting, retaining, and paying for the same information. These issues exemplify the challenges that must be faced in aiming for interagency identity data sharing.

As the federal government has sought to align its processes more effectively and to become more businesslike some of these obstructive traits have begun to recede in prominence. At the same time, legacy and fragmented system solutions remain, including those that perform IdM functions.

Another area of critical importance to IdM generally is that of standards. This subject is addressed in more depth below, but as specifically related to digital ID stores, the lack of government-wide standardization in the use of existing data elements across the federal government has significantly contributed to slow progress and low levels of adoption.[9] Work has been done in some important aspects of IdM standards, notably in biometrics. However, there is still much work to be accomplished to standardize all aspects of identity data storage and use.

The problems attendant to this lack of standards are amplified in screening processes, where information derived from intelligence, law enforcement, or even foreign sources may use various transliteration, spelling, or usage conventions. The possibility that such data may represent aliases, and as such are inherently unreliable, cannot be discounted. Even so, the basic issues remain — when such data, however fragmentary and unreliable, are collected, stored, and managed in

---

[9] The need for standards has been identified as a key IdM enabler (NECCC, 2002).

separate "stovepiped" systems. Any judgments or new information regarding the underlying individual that precipitate changes to the data set must be duplicated identically wherever the data are held, or else the records will diverge. Over time, one person may appear as two or more digital identities, each appearing to represent a different individual, increasing the chances of misidentification.

An identity landscape characterized by similar but unconnected islands of data in non-standard forms raises significant hurdles in many data management areas: information assurance, data quality, privacy protection, security, and resource allocation. In this environment, risks are manifold and likely unknowable in their entirety. These are risks not only to government itself, but to the people it serves. As noted, dependency on IdM-based processes to perform increasingly broad, and increasingly important, governmental functions is an accelerating trend. Thus, insecurity in this area places increasingly-critical outcomes at risk, including those associated with national security.

2.1.2 Global Telecommunications Grid

The Global Telecommunication Grid (GTG) consists of the public-switched telecommunications network (PSTN), various forms of Internet protocol (IP) networks including the current Internet, managed Enterprise Networks and other IP networks (e.g., converged services), and "cable" networks. It is the means to collaborate, share information, and achieve and maintain information security.

This network of networks can be viewed horizontally as a system of interoperable, or at least interworking, transport networks, and also can be viewed vertically as a system of widely differing application services riding on the transport networks. Identity services are supported by a heterogeneous collection of providers (some of which may also be transported to network providers) to a large community of nomadic users and access devices over a wide range of access technologies. The GTG is notional, and its implementation is uneven both geographically and technically. The interworking bridging functions, those that enable disparate systems to exchange identity information and reuse existing credentials, between all the networks and services have not been completely addressed, particularly in IdM.

Within the government, the Department of Defense (DOD) has long sought to define, build, and manage a set of services as needed to support its unique global mission needs. This is called the Global Information Grid (GIG) and is discussed in some detail in Annex D.

Historically, the information and technology-support systems of the various departments and agencies of the federal government were not designed or built to be interoperable. Security concerns associated with sharing data, incremental costs involved in engineering the systems to work together, and, as noted, the general absence of broadly-scoped technology standardization, all served to inhibit interoperability. Until quite recently, interoperability across organizations has been dealt with on a case-by-case basis.

The growing sense of need for collaboration between and among persons and entities which are geographically and organizationally distributed has paralleled the emergence of the technical means to achieve such collaboration. In doing so, it has become increasingly important to positively establish the identity of the IT systems — and their operators — involved in such interaction. As will be discussed below, this has influenced the direction of advanced technical standards efforts, including those focused on identifiability of systems components, as well as more traditional human areas, such as biometrics.

2.1.3 Applications

The Task Force desired to better understand how digital identities are being applied in programs within and across the federal government, and toward that end, conducted a two-part analysis: Review of Privacy Impact Assessment (PIA) documents, as filed for existing federal programs; and a survey of federal Chief Information Officers, via a detailed questionnaire circulated to members of the federal CIO Council. Detailed discussion of these efforts and their findings is found in Annexes G (data calls) and H (PIA analysis), respectively.

2.2 THE INTERNATIONAL ENVIRONMENT

A major difference between the international environment and the domestic federal environment is that in the global context there is no overall governing body that has the authority to impose a consistent IdM organizational concept on the wide variety of IdM organizations. Instead, interworking and interoperability between disparate IdM concepts and systems is achieved through consensus that is ultimately negotiated in international standards-setting organizations. The development and eventual global adoption of technical standards as needed to support IdM processes on interconnected IT networks is in the critical path to achieving the values and potential benefits envisioned here.

Within the federal interagency process, the State Department coordinates U.S. positions on IdM that relate to bodies created or chartered by governmental organizations. The most notable among these are the International Telecommunication Union (ITU), the International Organization for Standardization (ISO), and the Organization for Economic Co-operation and Development (OECD), *inter alia.* More detailed discussion of these groups and their efforts may be found at Annex J. Typically, U.S. delegations to standards fora include representatives from other interested federal agencies, as well as representatives from the private sector. Other standards work is conducted under auspices of international trade associations and various federal organizations serve as sponsoring coordinators.

2.3 IDENTITY MANAGEMENT AND CYBERSECURITY

From the point of view of the U.S. government, the pacing factor in the emergence of globally interworking international IT systems is the emergence and adoption of standards-based architectures that support the full range of government missions, functions, and professional concerns. These include the ability to identify systems, data, and individuals participating in the network, and related to that, the full range of cyber security issues. While a detailed discussion of the latter topic exceeds the scope of this paper, there are certain areas of clear overlap between cyber security, writ large, and IdM. These are briefly addressed in Section 5.2.2.

2.4 REQUIREMENTS

Specific recommendations will be provided later in the report. This section addresses the top-level considerations upon which any successful IdM system — and most especially those of the proposed future state — must be predicated.

2.4.1 Privacy

Today's key privacy issues focus on managing and protecting information about individuals, as well as maintaining the public's trust and confidence in the U.S. government. Informational privacy deals with the rights of an individual as it relates to information collected about them. nformation privacy analysis usually focuses on technology — how a particular type or implementation of information technology affects the information privacy interests of those affected. In their influential 1890 article on the subject of privacy, "The Right to Privacy," Samuel Warren and Louis Brandeis focused on the then-emerging technology of handheld photography and how the instantaneous collection of information about individuals without their consent affected their right to privacy. The same concern raised in 1890 about photography continues to apply today to the federal government's use of IdM technology.

2.4.1.1 Privacy Requirements

The chief statutory privacy protection for personal information held by the U.S. government is the Privacy Act of 1974. The Privacy Act applies to certain records about United States citizens and aliens lawfully admitted for permanent residence. The records must be contained within a "System of Records," which is defined as "a group of any records under the control of any agency from which information is retrieved by the name of the individual or by some identifying number, symbol, or other identifying particular assigned to the individual." 5 U.S.C. § 552a(a)(5).

Additionally, the statute defines a "record" as "any item, collection, or grouping of information about an individual that is maintained by an agency, including, but not limited to, his education, financial transactions, medical history, and criminal or employment history, and that contains his name or the identifying number, symbol, or other identifying particular assigned to the individual, such as a finger or voice print or a photograph." 5 U.S.C. § 552a(a)(4).

The Privacy Act imposes a number of requirements on the agency holding the records and provides a number of rights to the individuals whose records are being kept.

These are examples of certain Privacy Act requirements and rights that will impact IdM systems:

- There is a general prohibition on the disclosure of Privacy Act records without consent, with certain exceptions.[10]

- Agencies must publish notices in the *Federal Register* describing their Systems of Records.

- Agencies must maintain information that is accurate, relevant, timely, and complete, while keeping administrative safeguards on their System of Records.[11]

---

[10] Exceptions include disclosures within an agency to those with a "need to know," pursuant to a published routine use, at the request of the head of a law enforcement agency, for the health or safety of an individual, and pursuant to a court order. See 5 U.S.C. § 552a (b)(1)-(12) (2006).

[11] Agencies may exempt certain systems of records from some of the Privacy Act's provisions. See 5 U.S.C. § 552a(j) and (k).

- With certain exceptions, individuals have the right to access to Privacy Act records about themselves and the right to request correction of Privacy Act records about themselves.

- Individuals also have a right to file a lawsuit in federal district court to enforce the obligations of agencies mentioned in the above paragraph.

The second major statutory privacy authority is the E-Government Act of 2002. It also affords privacy protections for individuals with respect to IdM systems. Section 208 of the Act requires a Privacy Impact Assessment (PIA) to be completed by the agency for most information technology systems that collect, maintain, or disseminate PII.[12] PII is defined by the Office of Management and Budget as:

> "Information which can be used to distinguish or trace an individual's identity, such as their name, Social Security number, biometric record, etc. alone, or when combined with other personal or identifying information which is linked or linkable to a specific individual, such as data and place of birth, mother's maiden name, etc."[13]

A PIA is required to analyze seven factors:

1. What information is to be collected;

2. Why the information is being collected;

3. The intended use of the information;

---

[12] One exception to this requirement is for national security systems. The E-Government Act does not require PIAs for national security systems as defined by section 11103 of title 40, United States Code.

[13] Office of Management and Budget Memorandum for the Heads of Executive Departments and Agencies, M-07-16, "Safeguarding Against and Responding to the Breach of Personally Identifiable Information," May 22, 2007, Page 1, FN 1.

4. With whom the information will be shared;

5. What opportunities individuals have to decline to provide information or to consent to particular uses of the information;

6. How the information is secured;

7. Whether a System of Records is being created under the Privacy Act.

Agencies are required to publish completed PIAs on public Web sites to allow for transparency to the public about their collections of PII technology systems.[14]

Underlying the application of the privacy requirements of both the Privacy Act and the E-Government Act is a set of guiding principles, also referred to as "Fair Information Practice Principles" or "FIPPs."[15] These principles derive from the 1973 HEW Report,[16] which described them as follows:

- There must be no personal data record-keeping systems whose very existence is secret.

- There must be a way for a person to find out what information about the person is in a record and how it is used.

---

[14] The E-Government Act does not require the publication of PIAs containing sensitive, classified, or private information.

[15] The Federal Trade Commission provides a general overview of these principles on their Web site, www.ftc.gov, direct URL: http://www.ftc.gov/reports/privacy3/fairinfo.shtm.

[16] "Elliott Richardson, then Secretary of Health, Education and Welfare, named an Advisory Committee on Automated Personal Data Systems to make an intensive study of the impact of computer data banks on individual privacy. Its detailed report, "Records, Computers, and the Rights of Citizens," was published in 1973 and recommended the enactment of federal legislation guaranteeing to all Americans a "code of fair information practices." H.R. 16373 [the bill that became the Privacy Act] embodies the major principles of these recommendations as they apply to an individual's access to records in the federal government." H.R. Rep. No. 93-1416, at 7 (1974).

- There must be a way for a person to prevent information about the person that was obtained for one purpose from being used or made available for other purposes without the person's consent.

- There must be a way for a person to correct or amend a record of identifiable information about the person.

- Any organization creating, maintaining, using, or disseminating records of identifiable personal data must assure the reliability of that data for their intended use and must take precautions to prevent misuses of the data.

In 1980, the Organization for Economic Co-operation and Development (OECD) adopted Guidelines on the Protection of Privacy and Transborder Flows of Personal Data, which provide a framework for privacy that has been referenced in U.S. federal guidance and internationally. The OECD Guidelines present a similar set of principles in Collection Limitation, Data Quality, Use Limitation, Security Safeguards, Openness, Individual Participation, and Accountability.[17]

Application of these principles requires identification of information that relates to individuals and then assessment of how privacy protections should be applied to the use of that information. While the Privacy Act does not identify technology specifically as the primary area of concern the way the E-Government Act does, the IT-centric nature of today's business and government operations means that the majority of the time, the privacy analysis will start with this consistent foundation: an understanding of what information is connected with a particular type of technology or IT system, how that technology uses the information, the individuals who may be affected by that particular use, and the methods used to protect privacy. This analysis is driven by a determination of how information and technology are managed in a particular technology environment. Thus, in or-

---

[17] The OECD principles are available on the OECD Web site: www.oecd.org, (direct URL: http://www.oecd.org/document/18/0,2340,en_2649_34255_1815186_1_1_1_1,00.html).

der to assess the privacy implications of IdM, one must first determine how information related to individuals is used in an identity management environment.

The next step is to determine how information in general is used in an IdM environment. The final step is to determine the implications of how PII is used in an IdM environment and the privacy considerations that should be addressed when deploying IdM.

2.4.1.2 Identity Management Environment

The IdM goal is to manage information related to an identity, as part of a process such as screening or access control,to manage activities within the application that relate to that individual, while seeking to keep the data relating to them separate. The privacy goal is to ensure that PII is used in a controlled, purposeful, and lawful manner and in a way that minimizes the impact on an individual. To achieve both the IdM and privacy goals, one must first find a common element, something that is referenced by both the IdM technology and privacy policy. That common element is information — attribute information, specifically. Attribute information are characteristics or elements of information that describe their subject. For example, an attribute of a person might be height or hair color. Another attribute of a person might be an assigned number like a Social Security number. Other attributes related to a person might be information about a person's activities, such as when a person applied for a federally issued identification card.

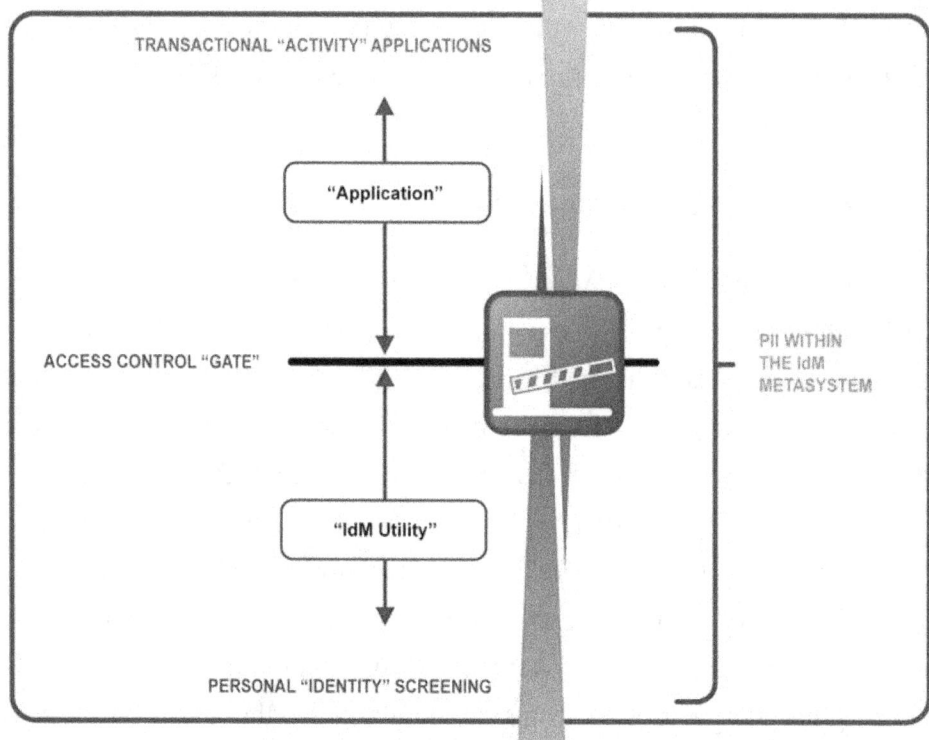

Figure 3. The Continuum of Personally Identifiable Information

Structurally, IdM can be viewed as the interaction of two sets of attributes, attributes about activities ("activity attributes") and attributes about the identity of an individual ("identity attributes") — managed by a control gate that associates identity attributes with activity attributes and enables applications to use identity information from remote sources. By viewing all the information in an IdM environment as attributes, one can more easily determine what identity attributes are required to support access to which activities within the application and then limit the use of identity attributes to only those that are required.

From a privacy perspective, all attributes should be considered PII and are differentiated by their location on the continuum of privacy sensitivity. It is impossible to gather enough information about a person to equal that person's entire "identity." Instead, there is a continuum of identity attributes that can be used either individually or in combination to point toward a single person as precisely as necessary. The greater the precision of the attributes, the more privacy-sensitive the attribute information becomes and the greater the privacy concern.

Because IdM will, by definition, use some identity attributes, there will always be some level of privacy concern. The issue will be the level of the concern based on risks to the individual and the organization. The more uniquely the attribute(s) identifies a person, or the more personal the quality of that attribute is (evaluated by the level of concern a person might have if that particular attribute were to be linked to that individual), the greater the potential privacy risk.[18] The greater the potential privacy risk, the more detailed the privacy analysis must be, and the greater the importance of privacy risk mitigations.

In addition to the privacy interest in identity attributes, there are also privacy interests in the activity attributes. In situations where an access decision is required, the application itself will use the identity information to grant access to specific activities and through that association, more characteristics of the individual could be created. For example, if the application tracks access to a sensitive government computer system, the record of gaining access to the system could also be a descriptive attribute of the individual associated with that granting of access. Here again, from the privacy perspective, there is a continuum of privacy sensitivity. Some activity information may be less privacy sensitive than others. When conducting the privacy impact assessment, however, one should always be sensitive to the context in which the information is used. Certain associations of identity and activity attributes may become more privacy sensitive based on the decisions about the individual that would be drawn from that combined information. In determining which attributes within an IdM implementation should be considered sensitive, both types of attributes, identity and activity, should be reviewed, and impact on the individual from the use of that PII should be evaluated within the specific context of the decisions made about that individual.

---

[18] In additional to specificity, other factors for determining sensitivity may include context of use, legal obligations, and combinations of different types and amounts PII.

The privacy analysis must address the full data life cycle — all uses of all the data by all the parties, over time — meaning that any activity data going back to the "source" of the identity attributes should be reviewed from the perspective of the organization providing the original identity attributes. It is possible that enough activity information could be sent back to the identity provider to give more information about the individual than was contained originally in the set of identity attributes. Any information that is used for the purpose of identifying and describing an individual should be considered PII and included in the privacy assessment.

The privacy impact of a particular attribute or a particular combination of attributes will always be context specific. Each use of each attribute that is linked or linkable to an individual should be reviewed to determine whether it is required to meet the specific needs of the application. Once that determination is made, specific privacy protections can be implemented to ensure that only those attributes are used and that they are used only for the specified purpose (that is, no additional information about the individual could be drawn from particular attributes information — both identity and application — that might extend beyond the original intended use).

Another key to a well-implemented IdM environment is a reliable trust model that enables the application to rely on the identity assertions of the identity provider. To prevent each application from establishing its own "identity" for the individual, applications must be able to trust the identity information they get from an identity provider. This trust makes it possible to isolate the specific identity attributes that are needed for the specific functions of the application. The infrastructure on which the trust model is based can then be relied on to support privacy protections to show that only specific attributes were used by specific applications for specific needs.

2.4.1.3 Privacy Protections

In any IdM implementation, and particularly as the use of IdM expands and more government services are managed electronically, fundamental privacy concerns must be addressed.[19] These include:

- Ensuring that the IdM-based service is designed with flexibility and implemented well to accommodate potential IdM changes. The design should operate the way it is described and improve security and delivery of the service without creating additional burdens.

- Supporting individuals who are not "in the system" due to financial status, difficulty gaining access, and other reasons. As "identification" becomes an increasingly electronic activity, emerging IdM systems might disenfranchise individuals that lack reliable electronic "attribute" information because they might lose the ability to participate in specific applications that functioned properly when relying less on electronic identification. Examples include victims of identity theft, for whom the identity attributes may exist inaccurately because they no longer point to the individual actually engaged in a particular activity. Avoiding the exclusion of such individuals is a fundamental necessity for an equitable system.[20]

- Upholding the accuracy of the data used by an IdM system is paramount, especially if matching programs compare data between IdM systems to verify user information. As a general matter, when PII is collected from the individual, the probability that the information is accurate is higher than when that same information is collected from a third-party source.

---

[19] For an in depth discussion of privacy issues related to identity systems, see: Peter P. Swire and Cassandra Q. Butts, "The ID Divide," Center for American Progress, www.americanprogress.org, June 2008.

[20] Ibid.

- Allowing individuals to maintain control of PII through user-centric IdM systems. If individuals insert PII directly into the IdM system, they may trust the operation of the system more because they know the nature and source of the information the IdM system is using to establish their access.

- Securing the core identifying attributes through encryption standards and privacy-enhancing technologies. When IdM systems rely on a set of core identity attributes, that core identity information must be secured to the greatest extent possible. This requirement applies to all PII, particularly when PII cannot be replaced easily, as is the case with biometrics. If PII is lost or otherwise compromised, established policies and procedures should ensure that data breaches are reported quickly and investigated thoroughly, and the affected individuals should receive assistance.

- Designing IdM systems based on open standards, using a flexible and interoperable infrastructure that spans numerous access devices and platforms. Such standards should support auditing by individuals and system administrators, encouraging consistent and shared responsibility to maintain accuracy and relevance of the information pertaining to the individuals.

- Preventing the identity attribute information from being used for purposes beyond those for which it was collected by using machine-readable policies that remain with individual PII attributes for the lifetime of those data to regulate access. Such measures hinder unauthorized use, and they could possibly send notification alerts to users and administrators of potentially fraudulent or inappropriate activity, much as credit file monitoring functions. In addition, these measures can deter possible "mission creep" within a particular system.

- Enabling individuals to access and correct information easily and verifiably in cases of identification errors within the IdM system. If individuals cannot fix errors conveniently and directly, the responsible agency/organization should provide a simple, effective, and verifiable mechanism for the individual to seek redress. The more privacy-sensitive the information in the IdM system, the more important these additional requirements become.

- Implementing privacy protections into the system so they are automated as much as possible but can be adjusted to accommodate new privacy requirements, as needed. Today, much of the privacy policy enforcement is accomplished through traditional methods, such as written policies and procedures given to system users to follow as they see fit. In the future, building protections directly into the technology will provide greater assurance that the protections are implemented thoroughly and consistently. That being said, there should always be a human-driven recourse to override the system when needed.

- Designing privacy training into the design and operation of IdM systems so system developers and users understand the responsibilities attached to using PII. OMB Memorandum 07-16, *Safeguarding Against the Breach of Personally Identifiable Information*, provides specific guidance concerning the training of employees (including managers) on their privacy and security responsibilities before permitting access to agency information and information systems.

- Removing PII when it is no longer needed. Retaining PII unnecessarily creates privacy risks. It should be noted that law enforcement and homeland security needs may require personally identifiable information to be held for investigative or screening purposes for long periods of time.

IdM, as with all emergent and evolving technology, will continue to present challenges to government and society to provide opportunities to reexamine fundamental principles, perspectives, and specific practices in new contexts. This point is constantly reemphasized over time, as public attitudes regarding a given program, technology, or process evolves. These attitudes will be heavily influenced by recognition of value and benefit, ideally packaged with convenience. Successful implementation of IdM for access control purposes should deliver real value directly to the individual including increased access to an expanded set of services, improved timeliness of service, reduced risk of fraud or error in the conduct of business with the government, and reduced risk of identity theft. The value and benefit of IdM will be enhanced by ensuring that privacy concerns are recognized and appropriate privacy protections are built into an IT system which uses IdM.

2.4.2 Policy/Authority

In addition to the laws discussed above, there are other authorities that also impact on the privacy and security of IdM systems. These include presidential directives, federal law, and Office of Management and Budget (OMB) guidelines. Among the former are:

HSPD-6, *Integration and Use of Screening Information*, was signed by the President in 2003. It seeks to "develop, integrate, and maintain thorough accurate and current information about individuals known or appropriately suspected to be or have been engaged in conduct constituting, in preparation for, in aid of, or related to terrorism." This directive was supplemented in 2004 by

HSPD-11, *Comprehensive Terrorist-related Screening Procedures*. This directive refines and expands screening processes.

NSPD-59/HSPD-24, *Biometrics for Identification and Screening to Enhance National Security*. This was signed in 2008. This directive "establishes a framework to ensure that federal executive departments and agencies use mutually compatible methods and procedures in the collection, storage, use, analysis, and sharing of biometric and associated biographic and contextual information of individuals."

HSPD-12, *Policy for a Common Identification Standard for Federal Employees and Contractors*, was issued by the President in August 2004. According to the Directive:

"Wide variations in the quality and security of forms of identification used to gain access to secure federal and other facilities where there is potential for terrorist attacks need to be eliminated. Therefore, it is the policy of the United States to enhance security, increase government efficiency, reduce identity fraud, and protect personal privacy by establishing a mandatory, government-wide standard for secure and reliable forms of identification issued by the federal government to its employees and contractors (including contractor employees)."

Additionally, several OMB policy memoranda have been issued in recent years that describe security and privacy rules for PII. These are in addition to OMB guidance on statutes like the Privacy Act and Section 208 of the E-Government Act of 2002. Since IdM systems by definition will contain PII, these requirements will need to be applied to IdM systems. Beginning in May 2006, OMB reminded agencies of their existing obligations under the Privacy Act to protect PII. Then, OMB issued memorandum M-07-16 that set forth additional security measures for information technology storing data and additional privacy requirements related to reduction of PII holdings and Social Security number usage.

The Information Sharing Environment (ISE)[21] is another initiative that has consequences for IdM systems. The ISE was created by Section 1016 of the Intelligence Reform and Terrorism Prevention Act of 2004, which in turn was based on Executive Order 13356,[22] *Strengthening the Sharing of Terrorism Information to Protect Americans*, Aug. 27, 2004 (subsequently replaced with Executive Order 13888). The Executive Order directed agencies to give the "highest priority" to the prevention of terrorism and the "interchange of terrorism information [both]

---

[21] http://www.ise.gov/

[22] http://www.whitehouse.gov/news/releases/2004/08/20040827-4 html

among agencies" and "between agencies and appropriate authorities of states and local governments." The President further directed that this improved information sharing be accomplished in ways that "protect the freedom, information privacy, and other legal rights of Americans." So, to the extent that IdM systems contain terrorism information, the rules of the ISE will apply, which include privacy guidelines that must be followed. IdM systems used for purposes of validating identity at border crossings will certainly be affected by the ISE rules.

The National Institute of Standards and Technology (NIST) has also promulgated standards such as the FIPS 199, *Standards for Security Categorization of Federal Information and Information Systems*, and FIPS 200, *Minimum Security Requirements for Federal Information and Information Systems*, that require agencies to conduct certain assessments of the information held in their information technology systems.

2.4.3 Standardized Expression of Identity

One issue touching on both policy and technical architecture is the lack of standardized ways to express "identity," as needed to verify users' claims to application access. This study has discussed "digital identities" and the essential role of these in any IdM system.

The fundamental problem today is that while there is well-defined policy guidance and technical specification for identity assurance levels,[23] there is no widely accepted process for defining and managing digital identities that supports requirements for different levels of identity assurance. Instead, there are many disparate and autonomous IdM systems that are based on locally established criteria. New ones are emerging all the time.

---

[23] OMB M-04-04, *E-Authentication Guidance for Federal Agencies*, December 2003 and NIST Special Publication 800-63, *Electronic Authentication Guideline*, April 2006.

A limited solution to this problem may be found in the concept of "federations." When a group of entities agrees to use a common IdM system concept, it enables these entities to share selected identity information about their users with others in defined trust relationships. Such a sharing arrangement is often referred to as a "federation." However, this approach has not significantly reduced the number of disparate identity systems worldwide. It may also default to the lowest common denominator of trust (and technical abilities, in some cases) among its subscribers. Sponsors sometimes deliberately keep participation requirements "loose" in order to attract more new adherents. Furthermore, as discussed elsewhere, there are some privacy concerns associated with federation that must be addressed.[24]

Notwithstanding its limitations, federation of IdM is an inevitable concept, unless one would seek to collect and store all relevant data within a single data environment. This option is not attractive to the federal government, in terms of either policy or technical practicality. Hence, it is accepted that interoperable cross-organizational collaboration is necessary, between and among data stores and data holders who are separated by organization, distance, and sometimes policy. For this purpose, an interoperable means of basic digital identification is essential. This must be common to all, and as rigorous as may be needed to support the most sensitive application of identity within the system.

The immediate challenge is the lack of interoperability between different IdM systems. Identity information needs to be exchangeable between IdM systems that use different technologies, platforms, protocols, data structures, and architectures. The ultimate solution is to develop a standards-based, universal bridging function that enables IdM systems and federations of systems to communicate with each other in order to achieve the level of trust required for any particular transaction. These concepts are discussed in greater detail in Annexes E and F.

---

[24] See R&D recommendation #2, section 4.3.1.

2.4.4 System Design

Many considerations may arise when managing and overseeing the identities of multiple entities, especially in large organizations. Following is a list of representative challenges that have to be considered within the execution of an IdM strategy.

- Complexity of task. The complexity of the existing IdM environment will make the task of mapping the data model difficult and extensive. As discussed, the current federal IT/IdM system lacks any overall concept or framework. Nonstandard development techniques; taxonomy, terms, and definitions; disparate system/process ownership will complicate any comprehensive census of the current environment.

- Complexity of the data model. In order to share data between these systems, it is necessary to engineer sometimes complex profiles (or data filters) to convert data from one system to a usable, compatible form into another system. Data structures and naming conventions are inconsistent. Same data is often represented by different field names. Differing database management service technologies can make data filtering problematic.

- System Interoperability/Interworking. This is conducted on any of several ad hoc models, which may vary according to local or transient needs. For this reason, the quality of system/configuration management may vary widely.

- Life Cycle management. Life cycle management refers to the establishment, proofing, modification, suspense, termination, archiving, and possible reallocation of identity data.

- User control of data. Any system involving human IdM may encounter conflict between the desire of systems and authorities to be able to identify individuals, and the desire of those persons to control the use of PII about them, specifically personal identity information. Future IdM systems must acknowledge and confront this issue, leading to solutions that meet all needs.

- <u>Organizational control of data</u>. The use of classic security technologies and IdM architectures (e.g., federation) may result in increased access to information stores, thereby leading to an increased potential for abuse. The use of simple anonymity techniques to achieve privacy protection leaves the system without auditing mechanisms that are required in many scenarios. This may cause a conflict between security and privacy that will leave neither party satisfied. In addition to the expectations of the users, relying parties (those who are extending information, privileges, goods or services to "identified and authorized" persons) also have expectations related to central authorities protecting their relationships with their users (e.g., to prevent exposure of sourcing arrangements between different vendors, suppliers, and customers).

- <u>Diverse Requirements.</u> The federal government has already promulgated several IdM systems employing diverse standards, some of which are large scale, (HSPD-12/FIPS-201, Transportation Worker's Identification Card (TWIC), First Responder's Access Card (FRAC), etc.). Beyond these identification card-based systems, there are prescribed ID frameworks established for the Health Insurance Portability and Accountability Act (HIPAA) and the Sarbanes-Oxley Act, *inter alia*. Finally, various international partners have their own laws, policies and public opinions regarding identification and privacy. It will be a challenge to produce a single IdM framework that can support all federal government requirements.

- <u>Ownership Issues</u>. Whether in industry or in the government, entities are usually reluctant to give up exclusive ownership of their data or to permit automatic access to proprietary data. The reasons for the reluctance are not necessarily the same for industry and government, but without trust, it will be difficult to provide access.

- Standards. The availability of needed technical and process standards, and their adherence, is foundational to the development of any large-scale IdM system. This will only be increasingly true over time, as the federal government seeks to increasingly interoperate with partnering organizations.

- Streamline IdM Systems. The implementation of IdM systems designed to leverage new identity credentialing programs (such as the PIV card for federal employees, First Responder Authorization Cards (FRAC) etc.), consolidate capabilities, or enable single sign-on processes may result in a reduction of the number of registrations and enrollments users are required to undergo, resulting in a decrease in the number of digital identities that users must maintain and providers must manage. However, single sign-on is a challenge in a nomadic environment where the access profiles must be available from random locations. It also may be a challenge because users have different roles in different situations. The challenge is to design an IdM framework that can support a single sign-on scenario while distinguishing between various roles that a specific user may play.

2.4.5 Taxonomy

As noted, one of the challenges in any effort to approach IdM is found in the proliferation of diverse taxonomy, as adopted over time by myriad legacy programs. Achieving consensus on a broad and adaptive taxonomy is in the critical path to overall success in harmonizing IdM efforts across government. See Annex K for the IdM Glossary used by the ITU-T international standards efforts, which is adopted here.

3 THE PROPOSED FRAMEWORK

This is a vision for a government-wide IdM framework. It seeks to define and describe, to the extent possible today, the values, priorities, and policies that such a development must uphold. It will do so in context of the dual interests of achieving the potential improvements, savings, and efficiencies inherent in IdM, while *enhancing* privacy relative to the status quo. In so doing, the major architectural elements of the future system, their relationship to each other, the data used within the system, and the various organizational and individual equities involved, will all be discussed. To this end, we make the following assumptions:

- Identity and the management of all the personal identifiable qualities of identity information are considered a critical asset in sustaining our security posture.

- To the extent available and practicable, a very high confidence in an asserted identity is recommended as the basis for authorization for access to government applications regardless of assurance level required. For example, PIV credentials required by HSPD-12 and used by federal employees and contractors are available and provide for a very high level of confidence and could be used for accessing all applications — even those requiring lower levels of assurance.

- There is an expectation that revocation of identity data and the related authorizations are executed in accordance with government-wide standards throughout all applications (whether used to support logical or physical access.)

- There is an understanding that management and protection of identity is not the responsibility of any one or a few federal agencies, but rather the responsibility of all federal agencies to enable. Identity is a component of each and every transaction. If one federal agency fails to carry out their responsibility, access to our networks and facilities will be significantly jeopardized.

The most important point to make at the onset of this discussion of "the future of IdM" is that it is not just about people. While the government is primarily concerned, as a matter of public policy, with the rights and privacy of persons in the context of IdM (this will be discussed at length in this report), at the same time, certain trends in technology must necessarily be accounted for in the course of the discussion. These trends will strongly influence the evolution of the increasingly-mobile IT architecture.

Both screening and access processing are discussed in this report. A primary difference will remain, however, as regards to the handling of PII in support of the two functions, and this will be discussed in some detail.

Finally, it is important to note that the proposed framework, described herein, is not a formal statement of policy that requires any action on the part of existing federal IdM systems without further guidance. The Task Force does not have that authority, nor have there been sufficient deliberations on the issue among the executive branch to take such a step. Rather, this discussion provides a common, learned foundation upon which to base those discussions in future.

3.1 THE GLOBAL TELECOMMUNICATIONS GRID

The future of IdM is predicated on the use of information technology to support human interaction, including providing the ability to conduct such interaction at a distance. This is done with the aid of terminal devices, which are components of the global IT infrastructure.[25] In recent years, there has been an explosive growth in the total population of these digital end-user devices, with a global population of more than one billion personal computers by the end of 2008 and two billion by 2015 being credibly forecast.[26] At the same time, the trend toward accommodating "nomadic" and mobile wireless systems as a growing percentage of that total has accelerated at a breathtaking pace — up more than 5,700 percent in the 18-month period between June 2005 and the end of 2006, for ex-

---

[25] "Global IT infrastructure" is being used as a generic phrase in this discussion. Internal government networks would thus be a subset of the broader global network.

[26] http://www.forrester.com/Research/Document/Excerpt/0,7211,42496,00.html

46

ample.[27] Taken together, these two trends lead to the conclusion that it is just as necessary for the elements of the network to be able to recognize, trust, interact and share information with each other, as it is for any given individual to be able to use such systems to reach a distant person, data store, or resource. A successful outcome can be achieved only if both the accessing systems and the persons using them can establish their "identities," and with that, their authorities and privileges.

Not only do the human-identifiability outcomes that define the functionality of the federal IdM system and the internal identity structure of the supporting IT "network of networks" have certain similarities, but they also possess unique features and qualities. Figure 4 summarizes the aspects of the total system that are unique to both human and technology domains and those that are necessarily common.[28] Later in this report, the concept of an "interface specification" between specific human-centric ID applications and the servicing federal IT system will be addressed. This graphic offers the first look at the underlying concepts supporting that assessment. Subsequent sections will address several of the points made on this diagram.

---

[27] *Networked Nation: Broadband in America, 2007.* National Telecommunications and Information Administration, Washington, DC, 2008. Pg iii.

[28] A new standards initiative of the ITU-T called X.1250, discussed in greater detail in Annex J, embraces this total domain.

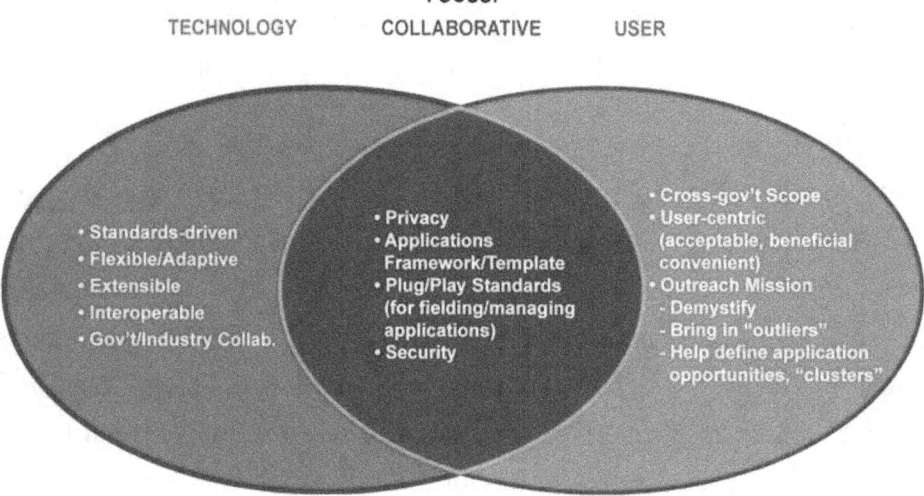

Figure 4. Comprehensive Approach to IdM

In IdM, as in other areas, technology systems are designed to support human needs. In that respect, the objective architecture for IdM in the U.S. federal government is predicated on several top-level goals and characteristics. These include:

- Configuration and operation of a "network of networks" to securely manage digital identities, based on a set of common data elements for stored PII that will allow it to be leveraged by a broad range of applications;

- Security of process, data transmission and storage. This includes and embraces all features of confidentiality, integrity, authenticity, and privacy, including use of encryption and multifactor authentication;

- Auditability of processes, with complete, automatic, and secure record keeping;

- Ubiquitous availability, at global distances, of strong verification of stored digital identity when called for or needed to support an authorized application;

- Standards-based connectivity, interoperability, and extensibility of supporting IT architecture;

- Preservation of application-specific PII data under control of application sponsors, with minimal exposure to unauthorized access or unnecessary transmission across networks;

- Ability of prospective application sponsors to develop, install, and operate applications in a way that permits the supporting IT grid to be seen as a freely available, ubiquitous service.

To the extent that these require development, refinement or adaptation, they will form the basis of Research and Development (R&D) requirements cited below.

3.2   "PLUG-AND-PLAY" IDENTITY APPLICATIONS

In the objective IdM system, the character of identity-based applications is very diverse, and the data they contain and use is often unique. This is the area in the total system, where end-user value is recognized, and application-level work is performed.

The way electric power is used in homes is instructed here as an analogy. This is depicted at a high level in

Figure 5 below.

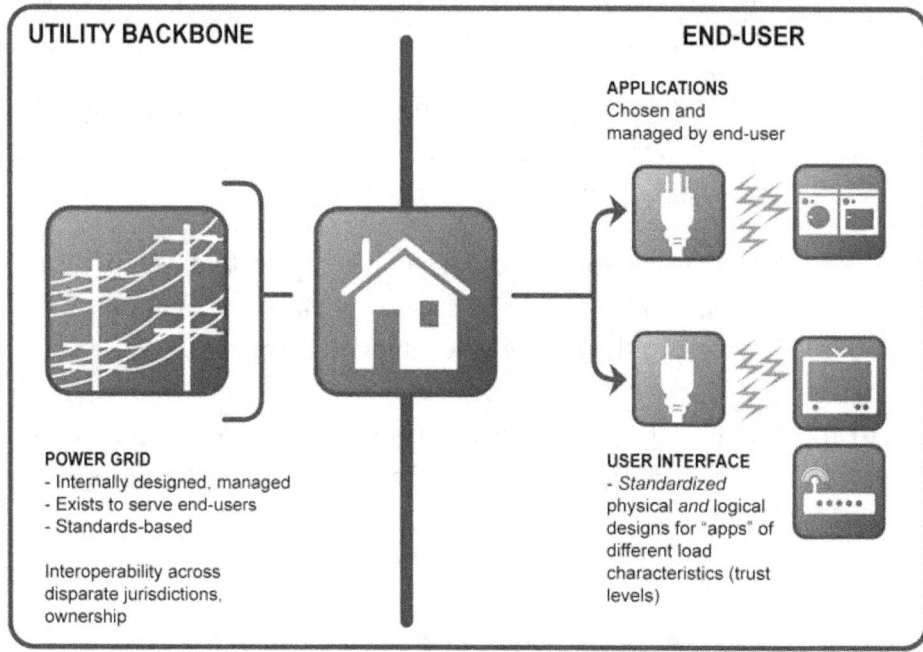

Figure 5. Electric Power Analogy

Within this model, individuals decide to select, purchase, install, configure, and operate electric power appliances in their homes, based on their own preferences, needs, and resources. Technology providers make business-case decisions regarding the design and marketing of new appliances to consumers and organizations, including federal agencies. In the process, they ascertain whether the device, by its nature, will require "low" (120 volt), "medium" (220 volt), or higher-level electric power to support its use. In all cases, the designers, vendors, marketers, and end-users are confident that the appliances will function in place, based on adherence to standardized specifications for interface with the servicing utility, which provides the capability to operate the devices at each of several standardized levels of performance — the electric power grid.

For its part, the grid is enormously complex internal to itself, with myriad entities, jurisdictions, regulatory bodies, authorities, and business arrangements.

However, it understands that it exists to deliver a suite of products, conformant to specifications, to the three-pronged outlets in the wall of all end-users — in the United States, 120 volt, 60-cycle alternating current. The utility also provides, in many cases, standardized product at 220 or even 440 volt levels, if the user specifies such a need (as for heavy appliances). These "interfaces" (plugs) have unique physical design characteristics appropriate to their use.

Viewed from the outside, the electric power grid is a complex singularity, not directly controllable by end-users. On the other hand, the grid can exert no direct influence on buying and operating decisions of end-users. Both know that their reliance on the other is predicated on mutual compliance with interface specifications and standards, within a set of business arrangements that are established and regulated with governmental oversight, in most cases.

The future federal IdM system can be seen in a similar light. The global IT grid may be characterized as a utility that exists to deliver defined services, while having no control over, or visibility within, the details or content of standards-compliant applications. Nonetheless, these applications depend completely on the servicing IT grid to provide identity verification of registered participants, and to conduct data transactions at global distances, with high availability, complete confidentiality, and confident data and transaction integrity.

In this context, identity application developers would be obliged to build to standards, for access to not only the data-transport process, as at present, but the larger federal IdM system. Through IT connectivity, these applications would be able to access stored digital identities inside the digital ID "network of networks." With adherence to these standards, the common elements of the federal IdM system would be freely available to applications, their developers, sponsors and users. At the same time, these "standard services" to support ID applications are offered at several different levels of trust, as appropriate to the need/nature of the specific application. The ancillary benefit is that exposure of the most sensitive, contextual application data would be restricted to the application and its authorized participants.

At the outset of this report, a simple model of the basic elements of the IdM system was displayed (Figure 1). Adapting that model to all subsequent analysis and discussion, the resultant model of the objective system is shown in Figure 6.

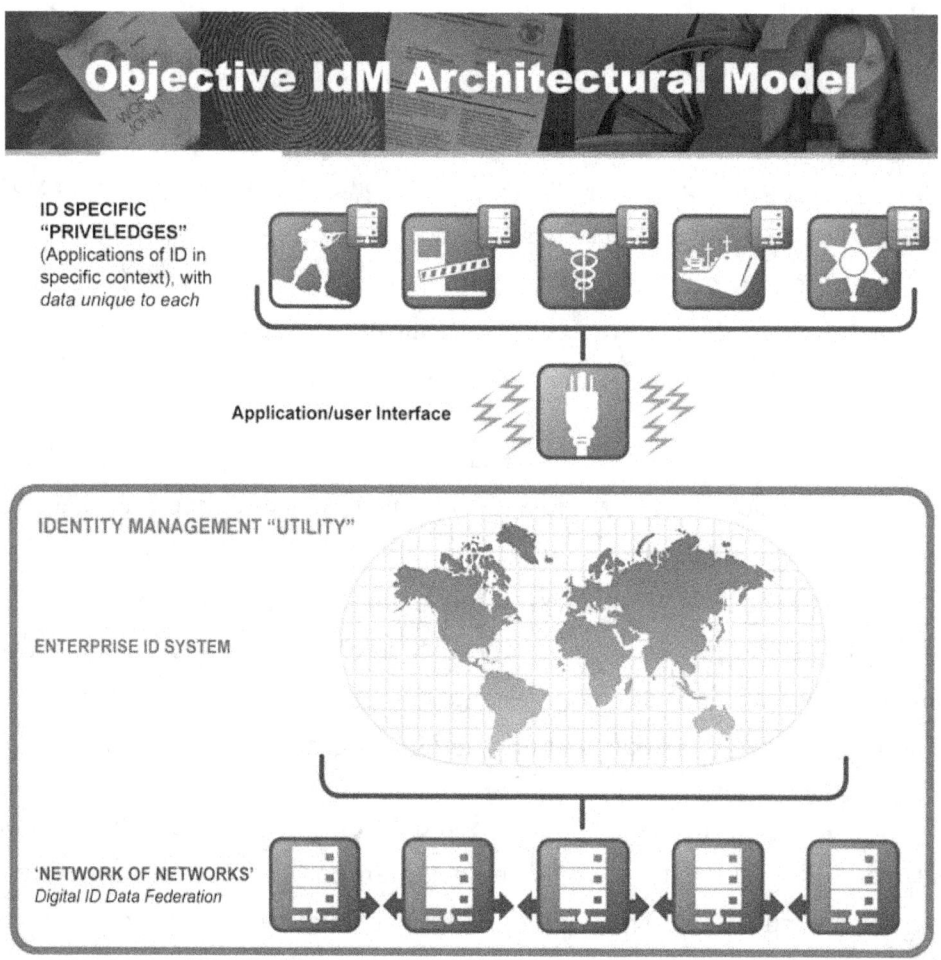

Figure 6. Objective IdM Architectural Model

In this environment, the business case for development and operation of new applications will be based on recognition of value and specific measurable benefit to the sponsor and the supported enrollees.

As implemented within the federal government, the value proposition for development of any new application can respond to any of several motivators:

- Legal compulsion (e.g., tax collection);

- Voluntary transition of traditional functions to more efficient means to perform the same purpose (e.g., making formerly print-based information resources available online);

- Creation of new functionality not previously available, based on:

  o Geography (e.g., telemedicine, medical robotics);

  o Scale (e.g., disaster response);

  o Emergent topical need (e.g., more stringent security controls in air travel to prevent terrorism; other applications to restore user convenience partly lost in the course of meeting anti-terror needs, e.g., to control access to government facilities or certain disaster areas).

3.3 DIGITAL IDENTITIES WITHIN A "NETWORK OF NET-WORKS"

Regarding data content and function, any IdM activity requires information sufficient to develop the digital identity of persons within the system. These data must conform to standards specified for use within and across the system. It has been noted that standardized ways of expressing these digital identities must be developed to promote interoperability. These must also be accessible, wherever located, as needed to establish and verify identity of persons asserting roles or privileges. However, these data need not be excessive and should certainly not express or reveal the contextual data associated with any specific ID application.

For example, if it is necessary to establish that a given person is John Doe, in order to permit him to view and work with classified information, this may be achieved by comparing some identity credential (user ID/password/PIN/ID card, etc.) in his possession; or biometric values (fingerprint, photo, iris scan, etc.) of that person to reference values collected and stored at the time Mr. Doe was enrolled in the system. If, an hour later, the same person then seeks to access healthcare, claiming to be an entitled beneficiary as a consequence of his federal employment status, the same interest in identifying him for purposes of verifying that "privilege" occurs, and possibly the same means may be used to do so. However, in neither case was or is it necessary to expose the contents or details of his participation "inside" these processes — classified information he works with, or details of his medical history — to confirm or deny his basic identity and access to the relevant privilege application. It is most certainly not necessary to expose these content-data specifics to managers of the other identity-related activity; all would surely agree that the two have nothing to do with each other, and would all find it an objectionable violation of privacy if that were to be done, most especially without the individual's knowledge.

Implicit in the foregoing point is the fact that there are multiple levels of confidence, or "trust," in the digital ID universe. These are, and will be, based on identity-proofing standards adopted by policy frameworks at the advent of development of a federated "network of networks" for interoperability. Also, different applications only require or request identity confidence to a specific level (based on policies governing them and other factors). In this regard, a conservative principle shall apply — only expose identity data (in the form of attributes) sufficient to support the needs of the application, and no further. In some cases, for some applications, users may be able to decide for themselves to voluntarily expose more or less sensitive private information, in order to access different levels of service.

There will also be differences in the level of identity confidence, as needed to support accurate authentication decisions, based on the use (or non-use) of supporting authentication mechanisms of three types:

- Something you are (biometrics);

- Something you know (PIN/password);

- Something you possess (ID card or similar physical token).

Ideally, the nature of the mechanism selected, and the way it is used, will be driven by the level of trust being sought at the application level. The combination of two or more of these authentication mechanisms may also affect the level of trust attributed to the identity assertion. Considerations related to scalability/management, user convenience, and security all enter into the decision process in this area.

In approaching this subject, the U.S. federal government has one huge advantage over most organizations. The existence of HSPD-12, as described, has provided a policy and standards basis for basic identification of federal employees, and some designated others, to a standard that is robust, interoperable, and mandatory across the federal establishment. The directive levels the bar across all federal departments and agencies, and sets it at a high level. This means that when the process of HSPD-12 adoption is complete across the government, there will be a rigorous basis upon which to predicate the kinds of applications development discussed above, using sophisticated mechanisms across the global IT grid to link the applications and digital ID stores. The HSPD-12 identity, however, does not apply to many groups and individuals that interact with government systems. It is these non-HSPD-12-identified individuals for whom further discussion and analysis will be required to determine how best to provide needed support.

Foundational work in this area was conducted by the federal government within the past several years, under auspices of the E-Authentication Initiative, as previously discussed. Of note, there are, and will continue to be, ID systems and applications that use authentication mechanisms (biometrics, userid/password/PIN, ID card), of various types, and often in combination. The objective federal IdM system must continue to accommodate this flexibility, while also striving to improve authentication implementations for all systems.

It has been established that digital identities, consisting of PII in the form of identity attributes, will be collected and stored in the digital ID Network of Networks. It has also been noted that work is needed to define common attributes and data elements that shall be taken to comprise usable identities and that these shall occur at multiple levels of rigor, matching various levels of trust in the identity of the person in question.

At the same time, PII will be generated and stored inside privilege applications. However, there is no reason why any PII will need to be accessed or shared for any purpose other than at the request of the individual it identifies. It is understood that these application-specific PII are often quite sensitive, in that they reveal aspects of the individual resources, conduct, and personal preferences of identifiable individuals. A person may be willing to share these in the context of a specific application, based on voluntary enrollment, where a perceived net benefit exists (e.g., reporting credit history on a loan application,). In some interactions with government, a person may be compelled by law to disclose PII, (e.g., earnings history to the Social Security Administration). The general case, however, is that individuals should be able to largely choose to associate with specific ID applications, and certainly know in which ones they are enrolled. OMB memorandum M-07-16, *Safeguarding Against and Responding to the Breach of Personally Identifiable Information*, provides additional guidance to federal agencies concerning the protection and use of PII.

Consolidating and streamlining credentialing of the federal workforce through HSPD-12, then leveraging PIV credentials as a principal means for accessing applications, provides increased security through two-factor authentication. Thus, two-factor authentication is among the highest priorities for IdM functionality *internal to* the federal government. In addition, it enhances the capability of single sign-on (SSO) solutions to ease the burden on the individual.

In discussing SSO within government, privacy goals are enhanced by ensuring the preservation of strong barriers between applications, in regards to the passage of PII between them. While it is possible to streamline the access of persons or entities to *accessing* multiple apps, it is essential that transactions *internal to them* remain unique to each and not be shared. In these ways, the convenience of SSO can be achieved within government use, while preserving application-level privacy. The commingling or sharing of data between applications is generally objected to on the basis that one application has nothing to do with the other.

Who we *are* is sensitive to us in *some* times and places;

What we *have, believe,* and choose to *do* almost *always* is...

This point is pivotal when both the scope and scale of the objective architecture are considered. A federal IdM architecture will and should be defined within the *scope* specified at the outset, which will necessarily extend across boundaries of jurisdiction (and thus, different laws and social views/cultures), technology approaches, nature of applications, etc. This architecture will not be "monolithic," but will represent a complex of disparate machines and processes, able to work harmoniously through development of, and adherence to, standards to achieve interoperability. This, in turn, would further support stronger privacy protections, because data governance policies can be developed and implemented — even implemented mechanically through physical control — at the data source where the context and purpose for collecting this information originated. The unique type of granular control is much harder to manage and confirm if data is sent from multiple sources to a single centralized location. ***It can not be emphasized enough that this centralized data store approach is NOT being recommended.*** The applications supported by this architecture will be enormously diverse, as will the nature of the content-specific data they use and retain (medical records, financial transactions, security clearances, data files, business records, etc.). At the same time, the *scale* of the object architecture will be global and massive, as needed to support the full range of federal government activities and enrolled participants. This latter consideration will inform architectural planning regarding design capacity and system performance under stress.

In Section 2, the current state of IdM within the federal government was described. Among the central conclusions, it was found that:

- There is much duplication of the collection and storage of basic identification data across the federal enterprise;

- The currently deployed architecture demonstrates considerable diversity in formats and standards of data element design and storage;

- In some cases, sensitive, application-level "contextual" data are exposed in transmission, or duplicated across applications.

In contrast to that, an IdM environment is proposed in which:

- Identity attributes necessary to support the development of digital ID are standardized to the extent possible;

- These digital identities would be stored within the IT architecture in ways that make them accessible by ID applications; they would be used for purposes of verifying identity upon enrollment, or assertion of entitlement to access a privilege application;

- Data associated with an individual's activities in any specific application would be held in and by the application sponsor, in what ever format was appropriate to that activity or the user convention in that application; in general, these would not be shared with other applications; their availability to any others would be governed by law and/or voluntary use agreement executed upon enrollment.

3.4 IMPLICATIONS FOR PRIVACY IN THE PROPOSED STATE

The case has been made that the current IT architecture consists largely of stand-alone, "stovepipe" systems, unique data paths, and duplicative PII repositories in diverse formats, often at the application level. As such, differences exist in the ways the same PII and other information are retained, portrayed, weighted, and valued across the total data architecture. Further, the existence of these duplicative and non-standard data increases opportunity for data exploitation and unauthorized access, and multiplies the likelihood that data will be stored, updated, and retained inconsistently across the architecture. These current threats to data integrity and privacy are summarized in Figure 7.

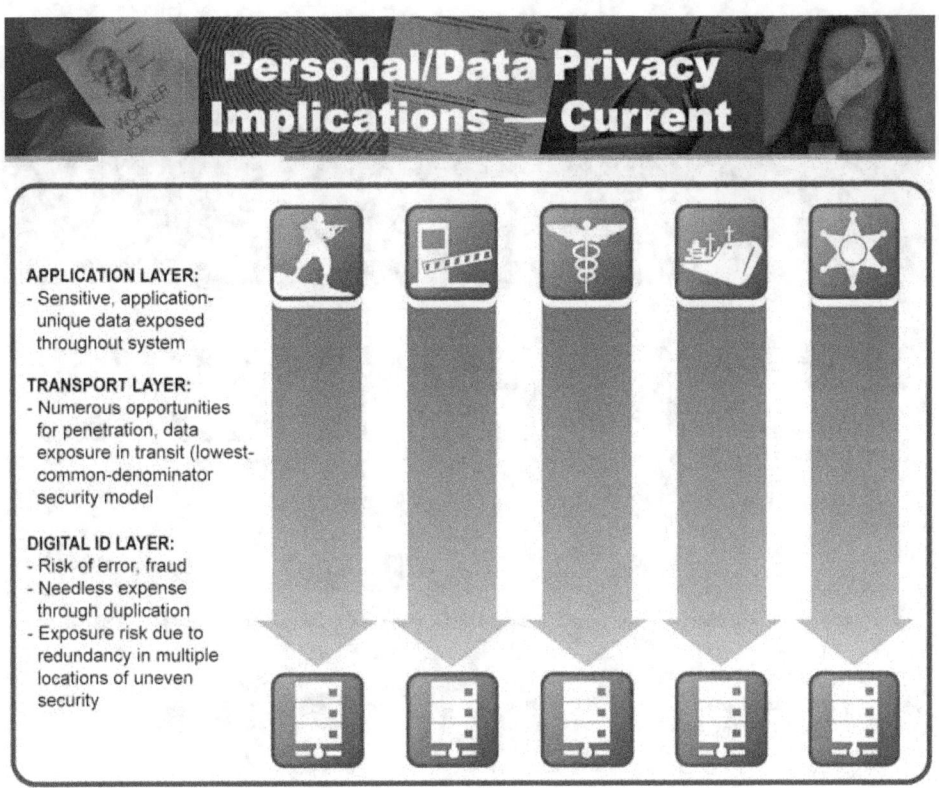

Figure 7. Privacy Implications of Historic Approaches to ID Architecture.

In dealing with these concerns, the Task Force postulates a federal identity implementation featuring much more commonality within and across the IT-service process, including cross-organizational and cross-domain interoperability within a scalable, federated "network of networks." This architecture would contain PII as required to support basic identification but not application-specific data. Individual applications would use a predefined process for querying data stores in order to verify a claimed identity. In so doing, the opportunity exists to envision a more privacy-sensitive approach to IdM, which should encourage the development and use of more and higher-performing identity applications. The effect of the evolved objective architecture, pertaining to privacy, can be made to look like the situation depicted in Figure 8.

The conditions depicted in Figure 8 suggest organizations seeking to develop or improve identity applications to perform their missions will be able to do so with confidence in the availability of an accessible, secure, and robust federal IdM system "at their doorstep." This will not only permit such organizations to achieve efficiencies and improve service, but to do so in ways that will improve upon the handling of PII and sensitivity to privacy issues.

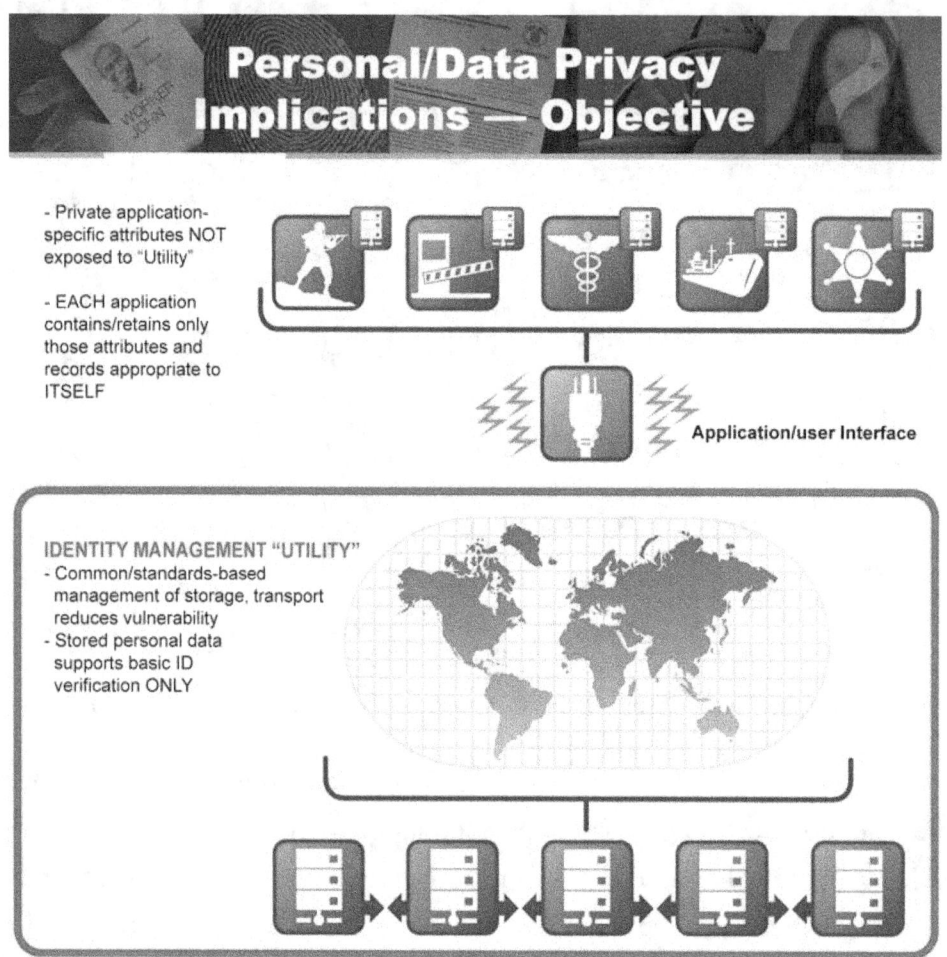

Figure 8. Privacy Concept in the Objective State of IdM

3.5 SUMMARIZING THE CHANGE OVER TIME

Many federal IdM systems today are completely unique in their approaches to technology, standards, and data management. This contributes to the complexity that has made IdM the purview of organizations and individuals with deep technical skills, and tended to discourage those whose only experience in the subject is that they have a job to do in the public interest, which either requires or will work better with a more effective and efficient IdM solution.

In order to achieve its full potential, IdM must evolve, over time, from being a domain reserved for expert technical practitioners, to the status of broad social acceptance as a useful and practical tool. In that regard, it is possible to envision advanced approaches to IdM as the critical path to achieving consensus on complex and important social issues.[29] By making the IdM process more accessible over time, the whole subject will be better understood by the public, thereby garnering increased acceptance and fostering industry development of entrepreneurial approaches that will result in improved end-use capabilities.

It is possible to achieve great strides in this area within the next few years. That assertion considers the state of development of technology; the extent to which IdM is being driven, in direction and pace, by threat-based factors, and the potential pace of public embrace of governmental identity-based programs and value-based capabilities. On the basis of those assumptions, the near future of IdM can be predicted as shown in Figure 9.

In the early days of the automobile, one needed a real understanding of internal-combustion engine technology to make a car start and run; today one need only turn a key, almost all of the time.

So it will be with IdM ... today's dauntingly complex technical processes will give way, over time, to invisible, ubiquitous service — the "dial tone" that is simply "there," ready to serve our needs ...

---

[29] See, *inter alia*,
http://energycommerce house.gov/Press_110/JAC.Report_FINAL%20Jan.3.2008.pdf, a Con-

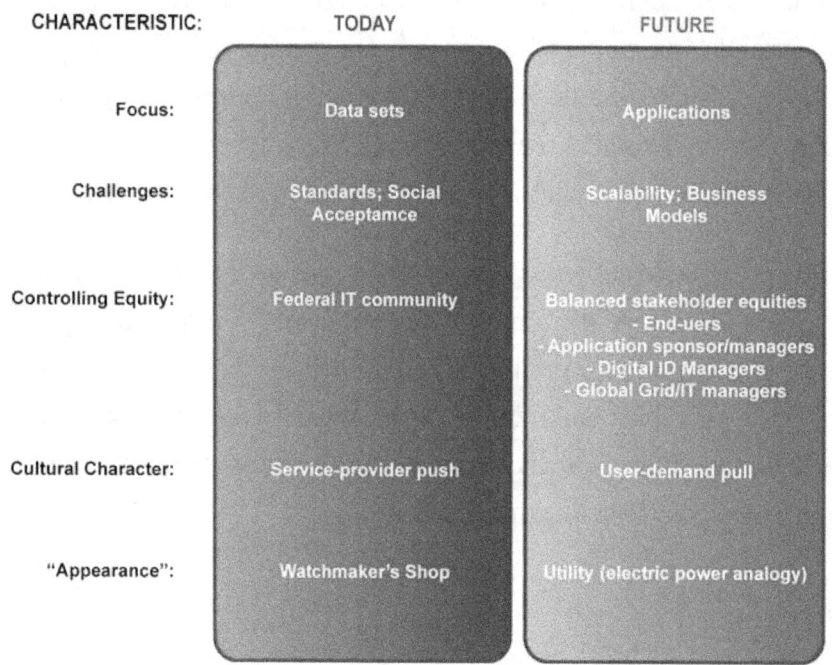

Figure 9. Federal IdM, 2008 vs. Future

gressional report on potential improvements in healthcare through use of advanced IT approaches and capabilities.

4 RECOMMENDED ACTIONS WARRANTING FEDERAL COORDINATION

As previously stated, this report provides a vision upon which to base a number of follow-on analyses and discussions. These will lead to the identification of specific policy and technology tasks. However, there are a number of agenda items that plainly need to be addressed, and that can be initiated concurrently, even immediately. In some cases, these will begin within a general discussion framework, and progressively becoming more specific over time.

4.1 STANDARDS & GUIDANCE

The development and management of the kind of IdM framework described here will not be possible without development, adoption, and adherence to a number of technology and process standards. Some of these have not yet been completed or ratified for adoption; in other cases, development has not yet begun. The Task Force considers this aspect of work to be among the most critical in achieving the potential value and benefits of IdM.

4.1.1 Standards Bodies

International standards will need to be developed over the next decade to implement the conceptual model of the global IdM framework described above. The U.S. will need to participate actively in the international organizations that develop these standards in order to ensure that non-federal IdM systems and federations of systems will be able to interoperate with the federal government's IdM system.

4.1.2 Application Format, Interface Specification

The success factors for a reliable and interoperable IdM system requires a framework consisting of standardized processes and technical specifications that are application neutral, extensible, standards-based, and adoptable by service providers, operating system vendors, application developers, and system integrators.

Minimally the specification should include a standards-based approach for the following:

- Identity Management framework;
- Application programming interfaces;
- Hardware token interface;
- Security architecture;
- Conformity testing;
- Authentication protocols;
- Capability discovery mechanism;
- Privacy enabling technology;
- Extensibility mechanisms.

The security architecture should specify levels of security to support varying user requirements.

4.2 ARCHITECTURE

Identity Management architecture should be consistent with two themes: the citizen-centric, line-of-business approach defined in the Federal Enterprise Architecture (FEA), and the wider architectural concept embodied in the city planning model.

The OMB is developing the FEA as a business-based framework for government-wide improvement. The FEA is a business-driven approach to identify opportunities to simplify processes and unify work across the agencies and within the lines of business of the federal government. The outcome of this effort will be a more citizen-centered, customer-focused government that maximizes technology investments to better achieve mission outcomes. Integral to the FEA is the use of digital technologies to transform government operations in order to improve effectiveness, efficiency, and service delivery.

> Upon migration to common government-wide solutions, agencies will shut down redundant systems which will not only save money but also free-up resources for agencies to better focus on achieving their missions.
>
> FY 2007 Budget, Analytical Perspectives Volume, p. 152.

The city planning model underlies the basic structure of internetworking. It describes how entities join together to form networks, how networks join together to conduct internetworking, and it lays out the fundamental infrastructure requirements needed to make these networks interoperate. FEA, and specifically its Business Reference Model, takes a cross-cutting view of government services in terms of their business functions. It can be thought of as defining the government as a business sector in a model city. Government services are grouped together in a logical way in order to facilitate organizational efficiency and citizen access.

IdM can address the gap between the general city planning concept and the service/business provision model of the FEA. To obtain the efficiencies contemplated in the FEA model, a set of common services must be provided that allow the enterprise-level services to function. The OMB, in its discussions of the federal architecture, describe a set of back office services, similar to those required to keep any business running, such as accounting or inventory management. Lying below these, and just as critical to business continuity, are the utilities that provide general services to all businesses. In a well-run city, this crucial layer includes plumbing, streets, and other basic services available to all. In the wider environment, where cities are connected over distances, the utility layer also includes things like highways, railroads, and satellite telecomm links.

IdM is one of the infrastructural components that permits a network of networks to operate, providing a basic service that validates claims of identity so that individual business applications can determine what privileges are to be granted to that validated identity. The IdM architecture proposed here transcends the existing (but nascent) state of federated identity management. Within-enterprise efforts have been ongoing, and several organizations are working on ways to articulate a standards-based approach to IdM. Among these are the activities of the Federal Identity Credentialing Committee (FICC) working with NIST to define the architectural components of a government-wide IdM solution. The needed outcome — a change from the status quo — has been described in the proposed vision.

4.2.1 Federated IdM Systems: A Network of Networks

Many models present themselves under the city planning paradigm of internetworking. The public power grid, municipal water, and sewer systems offer examples, as does the telecommunications system. Each was built by connecting local systems together. The present state of IdM is that the local systems have been built, but they have not been connected and subjected to a structured and verifiable process in order to realize a cross-organizational trust framework. Because of this, identity needs to be established with every local system to be used by a single entity. The key architectural questions that must be addressed are: how will these cross connections be made, what standards will govern the connections, what services will be provided, and what will the governance structure of the service look like? Section 4.2.1.1 will address these issues, but before proceeding, a general outline of the network architecture is in order.

The first round of human network building was characterized by the growth and development of discrete solutions, railways, pipelines, telegraph lines, etc. By the time the telephone system was being developed, it was clear that creating a new networked infrastructure to replace an old one is expensive, time-consuming, and potentially duplicative.

As networks are built, the characters of the applications that use them evolve. Simply stated, the number of such applications increases, while the nature of functions performed and services provided proliferate, with a common core of services evolving, but that are redundant and lack the necessary standardization. This is the situation we face in IdM today. These predictable characteristics inform our sense of the architectural and process improvements that will be standardized, extensible, scalable, and easy to design and use.

At first, the commercial Internet was dominated by small collections of static pages that communicated unidirectionally. Eventually, more sophisticated applications were launched that allowed business processes to be run using the network infrastructure. Using a shared infrastructure is clearly preferable in terms of time, effort, and cost to building or buying dedicated networking capacity, as had been done in the past. The IdM architecture being proposed uses the same type of approach to infrastructure, existing network nodes will form a distributed network by connecting to each other across a common networking infrastructure, such as that described in Section 3. The resulting network will use an overlay architecture strategy. Each identity data custodian will retain its own internal organizational structure. In practice, this is generally an enterprise network consisting of several nodes joined in a private loop. As part of an IdM internetworked service, each of these nodes will establish a gateway (set of tools and services) that enables it to request/respond to identity verification requests from other entities. The gateways will use standards-based components such that each gateway is functionally equivalent on the external internetwork-facing side, while being customized to what ever extent is required for interoperability on the inward-facing side. Section 4.2.1.2 discusses the necessary components and their orientation within the overall "network of networks."

4.2.1.1 Scope, content, and management

The scope envisioned for the network is U.S. federal government-wide. That is, services will be provided for all departments and agencies of the federal government and intended to support all federal missions. Thus, the scope includes providing services to citizens and other clients of federal systems, such as other agencies, non-citizens, other governments, and business. This will necessitate a clear distinction between the identity service the network provides and the application-specific services that user agencies develop and maintain. Details of the activities and functions that must be supported are described in Section 2.1.3, as part of the current environment.

Details regarding the required data exchange are a key issue that received much of the Task Force's attention. Content questions include: what is "identity," what is "identity management," and what facets of what ever it is that constitutes identity will be exchanged in a networked trust environment? By limiting the exchange of data to authentication protocols, such as encrypted password, PIN, cryptosequence, PKI signature, or biometrics, using two-factor authentication, and responding by affirmation or denial, privacy and data protection are considered.

Defining identity is highly challenging and quickly takes on the tenor of a philosophical discussion. For the purposes of IdManagement, however, identity is simply the collection of data which a repository uses to represent identities within a given information system. The term "digital identity" is used to describe this collection of data. However, each identity may be claimed, locally or globally, using a much smaller set of data depending on the authentication protocols. Authentication mechanisms query IdM systems concerning data related to a claimed identity, to which the IdM system will reply with "yes" or "no," indicating whether or not the information in the query matches the stored digital identity.

In common with other organizations that rely on standards bodies, the cooperative would appoint delegates to the appropriate standards organizations.

4.2.1.2 Integration of Components Within the Total System

In order for the separate components that make up the network to function cohesively, they require an integration framework. The current dominant approach to this problem is Service Oriented Architecture (SOA). The SOA style evolved from and is still closely associated with Web services. It is a loosely-coupled architecture that uses standardized middleware components to enable disparate applications to exchange information. The goal of SOA is to minimize reworking of existing applications, extend their useful lives, and expand their potential for reuse across an enterprise.

As SOA emerged in the early 2000s and applications were beginning to be accessed across enterprises, the issue of authentication took on increased prominence. The ability to have users sign-on once and be able to access all of their authorized enterprise applications was obviously needed. The desirability of an "identify once, authorize many places" model is, in fact, a key driver of identity management initiatives.

SOA was originally developed for use within enterprises as somewhat narrowly defined. The goal was to create a way for organizations to tie together the many stove-piped applications that made up their information systems' portfolios without having to rewrite them to a common hardware/software platform. SOA is a solution to application proliferation in an environment of varying levels of expertise, deep repositories of legacy applications, and constantly changing infrastructure. As its name implies, SOA is a style, or approach, to information systems enterprise management. Although it is frequently associated with Web services, they are not identical, and SOA can be implemented with a variety of methods inside an enterprise.

SOA was not targeted at internetworked applications, primarily because they essentially did not exist at the time. Instead, SOA has facilitated the birth of specialized networks of networks that ride on top of a commercial (or other) network. In this context, the possible configurations of SOA are more limited, as a Web services model is the only practical alternative.

An SOA/Web services architecture is still emerging, although significant work has been done to define and standardize the service model. Technical details of SOA implementation are beyond the scope of this document, but will play an important role in the success of an IdM Network.

It must be noted that SOA is not cost-free. Implementing an SOA gateway requires significant technical expertise, but even more cost is involved in the overhead that SOA imposes on transactions. Because of this known limitation, stringent performance testing is a necessity.

Importantly, SOA has some very desirable features that can be put to great advantage for IdM. There is the ability to pass extremely critical information from an entity through the privilege application in encrypted form without exposing critical information, such as authentication protocols. This information can only be read by the authoritative source for the identity, which is known via discovery. The IdM system, which can read the data, is authoritative for the identity claimed, and it can provide verification of the identity securely back to the relying party application.

This capability will totally defeat the phishing attacks that make use-rid/passwords/PINs so vulnerable. Even if a user is duped into passing information, such as a password, PIN, cryptosequence, PKI signature, or biometrics, the phishing application has no way of reading the data, making the attack pointless.

4.2.2 Security Within the Architecture

Adding further to the discussion in section 2.1.4.2, the converged IT and IdM-support architecture will require the full suite of technical, polic,y and process protections traditionally associated with Information Assurance or cybersecurity, and those demanded by law, policy, and public opinion that regard the protection of personally-identifiable information.

In many application contexts, and certainly in that of IdM, it is important to protect the content of messages exchanged within and across networks. The role of security varies according to the risks involved in the communication transaction. Because IdM brings with it risks on many levels (individual, governmental, and even global), security is a principal function that must be provided by the system. Security measures can be provided at any layer within a communications network, from the composition of a message, through its packaging, emission, carriage, and reception. Security requirements invariably impose constraints on design choices, just as the needs for interoperability and scalability do.

The Internet, as a whole, has high levels of interoperability and scalability. Until recently, with the advent of DNSSEC and IPv6, its security has always been of lesser prominence as a design feature. The Internet is a distributed model, a true network of networks that possesses no centralized structure. All points are connected to all other points through a distributed set of routing tables and switches. Consequently, security measures must be distributed, as well. In practice, this means that entities that are connected to the network begin by protecting themselves at the network gateway. In the city planning model, network perimeter security may be thought of as the gates and moat of a medieval town, while the roads leading to the town are the common network infrastructure. Depending on the security needs of the city's occupants, there will be varying methods used within the city walls. The town's bank and armory will be heavily secured with thick walls and guarded doors, while the individual residents may choose not to even lock their houses. The level of security required depends on risk profile and cost structure.

In addition to these measures, the federal government is currently engaged in a major effort to address cybersecurity, much of which is out of scope for our discussion here. However, there are several areas of overlap between cybersecurity and our work in IdM, for instance:

- Standards-based interoperability and connectivity across organizations and data environments (see also Annex J);

- Research & Development (see also section 4.3.1);

- Situational Awareness – the ability to continuously know the status of the security of systems and their data across broad architectures (see also section 5, recommendation #6);

- Education & Outreach — The ability to educate system designers, users, and the public regarding the needs for and benefits of IdM; at the same time, the same audiences must be made aware of the imperatives to adhere to standards whenever possible, especially those that support the safe and secure handling of personal information (see also section 5, recommendation #7).

4.3 S&T CONSIDERATIONS

Science and Technology recommendations are summarized below, in order of priority of the perceived need.

1. Public Key Technology. Public key technology, based on asymmetric key encryption, is a robust, cryptographically based IdM tool that has the power to provide strong identity authentication/access control, transaction integrity, technical non-repudiation, and an enabler for confidentiality. Its use today is closely linked to individual or group identity and the use of protective devices, such as hardware tokens, to ensure the protection of the private keys.

   While much attention has been paid to the infrastructure that supports generation, issuance, and life cycle management of the certificate services associated with public key technology, the protection of the systems and applications in which the technology is used have been less thoroughly examined. In addition, there is the need to explore public key technology in the context of anonymity — those cases where an individual's identity is less important than his or her privilege as a member of a particular group.

   Finally, the effective extensibility of this technology to a broader community has yet to be fully tested. As currently deployed, public key technology is largely used by governments and business entities in closed finite systems. While interoperability between these systems has been a core activity of policy and governance groups for the past decade with some level of success, there is a question concerning continued growth of the infrastructure and improving the interoperability processes in order to include unaffiliated individuals as consumers of this technology.

   As the public key technology presence continues to grow, the R&D needs can be categorized as follows:

   - Identify the tools needed to enable seamless use of public key solutions in existing (legacy) applications and systems with an emphasis on ensuring the end to end integrity of the transaction;

- Explore alternatives to hardware token-based (smart card) security for protecting cryptographic keys associated with public key technology, while preserving portability;

- Develop processes for the use of public key technology in protecting anonymity while preserving authorization/access control/transaction integrity;

- Investigate emerging capabilities for making public key technology more accessible and easier to use by a greater part of society;

- Investigate capabilities for ensuring the enhanced manageability (costs and effort required) of public key technology within and across the full scale (community size and demographics) and scope (diverse domains and applications) envisioned in this report;

- Explore advanced approaches to public key security and architecture which could lead to greatly enhanced performance over time.

2. <u>Privacy</u>. Within the context of IdM, preservation of privacy in a federation of IdM systems is particularly important. Several entities are involved in the IdM model presented in this report: providers of identity attributes, hosts of applications and the activity attributes, and entities that provide or manage access between the identity and the applications providers. In any given IdM implementation, PII can exist across both the identity and activity attributes and thus the entire environment must be analyzed for privacy compliance. The challenge is to build the IdM environment in such a way that minimal amount of identity attribute information can be used only when specifically needed by an application, and the overall creation and use of PII can be identified and addressed from a privacy perspective. Specifically, there are three related R&D challenges:

    a. Determine how to tier identity attribute information used within an IdM environment and standardize levels of privacy sensitivity of the attributes from a single core — perhaps highly privacy-sensitive — to a series of other attributes that have lesser privacy sensitivity. A tiered-approach to identity attributes will enable IdM implementers to view identity attributes along a continuum and to pick the appropriate level of identity information to support the particular application and, through these choices, to minimize the use of PII and provide greater privacy protections;

b. Determine how to tier the access control environment to enable the mechanical association of specific identity attributes from the continuum of privacy sensitivity described above with the specific needs of an application, and potentially use that same control mechanism to govern information about the application back to the identity attribute provider;

c. Determine how, in a standardized way, to actually construct an IdM implementation that aligns tiered identity attributes and tiered access control that could regulate the level of privacy sensitive identity attribute information required to support access to a particular element of the application, and to do so in a federated IdM environment; he IdM implementation would enable control over identity attributes to remain with the identity provider, while control over the activity attribute information would remain with the application provider and thereby provide privacy protection for PII across the entire federated environment.

3. <u>Digital Identity Network of Networks</u>. The objective architecture of networked and interoperable digital identities described here will require the discovery, standards rationalization, and integration of such holdings across the federal government, all while designing auditing processes and security safeguards to guarantee privacy in transaction and data storage. At the same time, specific data elements and standards for these must be developed as required to support digital identification. It is important to repeat that these must be comprised of minimal common PII attributes to the extent possible. An early example of the use of data elements to support digital identification is the

Personal Identity Card (PIV) mandated by HSPD-12 and described in NIST FIPS 201. While this model is appropriate for internal U.S. government use, different approaches must be pursued for enabling external communities of interest. In addition to developing a technical approach for external interaction, research will be required into the socialization aspects of the identified solutions.

4. <u>Identity applications interface</u>. As discussed, the goal is to permit potential designers and users of applications to think of — and treat — the servicing IT backplane as a utility, whereby services are predictable in terms of availability, nature, and performance. This will require that the interface between end-user systems, work environments, and the identity-management-support functions of the core network be defined in standardized terms. This will lead to development of applications more sensitive and responsive to specific user requirements, while facilitating the safe, secure, and efficient management of ID-support functions across the IT backplane. Some research is required to further define and develop the technical specifications to permit ID applications to "plug and play" into the federal IdM system at multiple levels of trust, as appropriate to/needed by the application, via the global IT backplane.

5. <u>Secure authentication</u>. This is used to identify entities that interact with an IdM system. These may include cryptographic challenge-response protocols, pass phrases, or biometrics. R&D is needed to find new methods of authentication or combinations of existing methods that are robust against attacks, such as password guessing, code cracking, or man-in-the-middle attacks. Authentication methods should also resist denial-of-service attacks in which a legitimate entity can be locked out of an IdM system by a malicious user. This research must be applicable to implementation in supporting card/token-based, as well as cardless, IdM authentication mechanism.

6. <u>Scalable authentication mechanisms</u>. The end-state IdM framework will challenge traditional approaches and concepts in authentication. To prevent costly errors and lost time, research must be conducted in anticipation of very large-scale IdM implementations, with extensive remote access capabilities. Design features must take into account the necessity to grow as the community grows while maintaining the trust environment. Identity proofing, enrollment, life cycle management, and other factors related to operating a successful IdM system should be anticipated, modeled, and proven. In addition, the diverse nature or scope of potential applications must be anticipated in system and architectural design, and factored into designs for latency, system loading, and throughput. The end-state authentication processes must be extensible, adaptive, and externally auditable, to ensure public trust and system integrity.

7. <u>Biometrics</u>. This is a topic that has grown in significance in recent years. In general, the passage of time, plus dedicated attention and study, has served to demystify this subject, while rationalizing performance claims.[30] Since they do not depend on either the possession of any physical object or the memorization of detailed user ID/passwords/PINS, biometrics may offer a potentially attractive option to strongly authenticate the identity of persons who have been previously enrolled in ID management systems designed to use them. However, the use of biometrics in unattended or remote applications is still a cause of debate within the computer security community. There is much work still to be accomplished in this area to ensure biometrics are used appropriately. The two reference studies cited identify numerous R&D needs in this area, and these are endorsed as written.

---

[30] Biometrics have been studied in some detail by government in recent years. See The National Biometrics Challenge (http://www.biometrics.gov/Documents/biochallengedoc.pdf); and the Report of the Defense Science Board Task Force on Biometrics (http://www.acq.osd.mil/dsb/reports/2007-03-Biometrics.pdf).

8. <u>Federation with systems outside the federal government</u>. IdM systems used by the government are expected to interact with a federation of other systems used by state and local governments, tribal administrations, and foreign powers. To ensure privacy and security of the government IdM systems, we must manage the interactions within the federation based on an understanding of the policies and practices of the other systems with which we are sharing trust. Research and development is needed on tools and techniques for expressing, comparing, and composing IdM policies and practices across these disparate architectures.

9. <u>Supply chain management</u>. The design and validation of hardware and software components of IT and IdM systems present a serious area of system vulnerability if not examined and dealt with. The increased dependence on such systems in the future will demand a level of trust in IdM systems that is generally greater than our trust in computer systems today. Research is needed to develop mechanisms to permit the confident embrace of technology components within IT and IdM architectures, with minimal concern for insecurity based on the components themselves or their sources.

10. <u>Security Vulnerability Analysis</u>. IT system hardware and software interact with the social network of administrators and users. As systems hardware and software design are progressively improved over time, attackers will continue to seek the softest point of entry to penetrate and compromise critical processes. Improved IdM processes can mitigate many of these vulnerabilities

11. <u>Usability</u>. There will clearly be more sponsors, managers and end-users embraced within the future federal IdM system. Research is required into enhancing ease of public access and use of these systems. Incorporating the principles of human systems integration will endure

improved system performance as well as user understanding and utilization.

4.3.1 Urgency

The prioritization of R&D work related to this report is as indicated in the numbering system used, with lower numbers denoting higher priority need. Beyond that, the general speed with which IdM is being deployed globally will demand urgent and sustained U.S. federal attention to this subject. This report seeks to develop a comprehensive picture of needs and opportunities related to IdM. Failure to see the process in the scope laid out here will lead to underperformance, relative to both achieving potential and meeting pressing needs.

4.3.2 Use and Misuse

Any attempt to compile a complete list of the operational and mission requirements of the entire federal government for identity-related applications would be a very extensive undertaking. Any such list would grow continuously, and as the standards, developmental, social and policy activities discussed here advance, the pace of such progress will only accelerate.

Representative use cases from some federal organizations participating in this work can be found at Annex I. Also in that Annex are "misuse cases." These are examples of behavior that should be detected, deterred, and prevented through technology and policy efforts.

4.4 GOVERNMENT-WIDE COORDINATION

As noted in Figure 6, the objective IdM architecture features a management framework wherein equity is distributed across every major component of the federal establishment. This is because every organization will design, develop, field and operate ID applications within its own purview, with co-dependency on the global grid and digital ID processes as service providers. At the same time, this report has sought to make the case for the value of standardized processes to permit streamlined workflow across the federal enterprise. Some of the complexities and challenges associated with achieving these goals have been identified.

The effect of this will be a continuous need for horizontal interaction and coordination across the federal interagency environment. This need will be particularly acute in early years, as the components of the federal IdM are conceptualized, designed, developed, rolled out, and tested, eventually displacing legacy systems and procedures.

Therefore, an enduring IdM forum comprised of existing federal initiatives concerned with IdM activities and operating under the overall guidance of the EOP, should be empowered to help facilitate the further design, development and use of Identity Management across the federal enterprise. This body would coordinate with the individual efforts of the various departments and agencies, as these seek to enhance their own systems and capabilities in this area, identifying gaps across these existing activities and work to overcome those gaps. The interagency focus would emphasize: cross-organizational interoperability and architecture; development and adoption of standards; use guidelines; and development of consistent legal and policy approaches to IdM across the federal government in the performance of all of its missions.

Representative Federal IdM Coordination efforts include:

- Federal CIO Council, under whose leadership the following activities are chartered:
    - Federal Enterprise Architecture Committee
    - Federal Identity Credentialing Committee
    - Federal PKI Policy Authority
- Committee for National Security Systems
- NSTC Subcommittee on Biometrics and Identity Management
- Information Sharing Environment (ISE) Identity and Access Management Initiative
- President's Identity Theft Task Force
- Terrorist Screening Center
- ODNI Interagency Identity Intelligence Task Force

Annex A Task Force Charter

CHARTER

of the

TASK FORCE ON IDM

SUBCOMMITTEE ON BIOMETRICS

AND IDM

COMMITTEE ON TECHNOLOGY

NATIONAL SCIENCE AND TECHNOLOGY COUNCIL

A.   **Official Designation**

The Task Force on IdM (TF) is hereby established by action of the Subcommittee on Biometrics and IdM (Subcommittee) of the Committee on Technology (COT) in the National Science and Technology Council (NSTC).

B.   **Background**

In recent years, electronic identities have proliferated rapidly, playing a key role in commerce, security, and many other aspects of today's highly connected mobile world. This change has been accompanied by an increased need to ensure high-confidence identification of specific individuals, giving rise to the confluence of biometrics and "IdM" (IdM).

Numerous IdM technologies, standards and related plans are being developed independently at the application and sector-specific levels (such as telecommunications, border security, financial services, identity theft, etc.). While these all positively contribute to advancing IdM, the technology and its potential benefits will be limited without cross-sector and cross-application coordination and a common technological foundation. At the federal level, needs and uses vary significantly, and a one-size-fits-all technical IdM architecture cannot satisfy all agency constraints and requirements. However, there are clear commonalities that would benefit from a coordinated federal effort, enhance agencies' abilities to meet mission needs, ensure privacy protection, and enable individuals to exercise their identities securely. In recognition of these challenges, the Subcommittee's mission was expanded in 2007 to include coordination of federal IdM activities.

C.   Purpose and Scope

The purpose of the TF is to assess the status of and challenges related to IdM technologies and develop recommendations regarding the federal government's science and technology needs in this area.

For the purposes of this Task Force, "IdM" means "the combination of technical systems, rules and procedures that define the ownership, utilization, and safeguard of personal identity information. The primary goal of the IdM process is to assign attributes to a digital identity and to connect that identity to an individual."

D.   Tasks

The TF serves as part of the internal deliberative process of the NSTC. Reporting to and directed by the Subcommittee, the TF shall:

- Inventory and Baseline IdM Activities, Applications, and Challenges.
    - Gather existing IdM-related information (such as documented needs, business cases, definitions, standards, plans, etc.) from programs/sectors of interest;
    - Review disparate IdM taxonomies across the federal government, and establish a common cross-sector taxonomy for standard usage;
    - Inventory ongoing and upcoming federal IdM programs to establish a current baseline of activities and needs, within the context of the common taxonomy described above;
    - Perform an initial review of federal, national, and international IdM standards activities, including intra-governmental coordination between the various centers of standards management and authority;
- Identify activities that warrant federal coordination.
    - Identify critical IdM issues that require immediate attention and action.
    - Identify issues that require long-term coordination, for example:
        - RDT&E (technology-specific, and in general)
        - Standards Development and Adoption
        - International and public-sector liaison
        - Outreach/Communications
- Develop recommendations for Subcommittee consideration.
    - Recommend changes to the Subcommittee's organizational structure to support necessary IdM tasks;
    - Propose a plan for the Subcommittee's subsequent IdM work;

- Identify necessary tasks that are beyond the subcommittee's purview and the groups best suited to address them.

E.   Membership

The co-chairs of the Subcommittee, working with the Subcommittee's existing Department Leads, will identify participants in the TF. The following NSTC departments and agencies shall be represented on the TF:

Department of Commerce

Department of Defense

Department of Energy

Department of Health and Human Services

Department of Homeland Security

Department of Justice

Department of State

Department of Transportation

Department of Treasury

Department of Veterans Affairs

General Services Administration

National Science Foundation

Federal Trade Commission

The following organizations in the Executive Office of the President may also be represented on the Subcommittee:

Office of Management and Budget

Office of Science and Technology Policy

The Subcommittee co-chairs may, from time to time, designate additional representation from other executive organizations, departments, and agencies.

The TF, upon receiving approval from the Office of Science and Technology Policy, may utilize the Science and Technology Policy Institute to provide assistance in meeting these tasks.

F.   Private Sector Interface

The TF may seek advice from members of the President's Council of Advisors on Science and Technology and will recommend to the Director, Office of Science and Technology Policy, the nature of additional private sector advice needed to accomplish its mission. The TF may also interact with and receive ad hoc advice from various private-sector groups as consistent with the Federal Advisory Committee Act.

G.   Termination Date

Unless renewed by the Subcommittee co-chairs prior to its expiration, the TF shall terminate on July 1, 2008.

H.   Determination

I hereby determine that the formation of the Task Force on IdM is in the public interest in connection with the performance of duties imposed on the Executive Branch by law, and that such duties can best be performed through the advice and counsel of such a group.

Final signature/date: 8 January 2008

Annex B Task Force Composition

Task Force Co-Chairs:

Duane Blackburn, OSTP

James Dray, NIST

Judith Spencer, GSA

Team Leads:

Bill Brykczynski, STPI	Data Collection and Analysis
James Ennis, DOS	Global Telecommunications Grid
Deborah Gallagher, DHS	Digital Identification
William Gravell, DOD	Report Drafting
Niels Quist, DOJ	Privacy

Task Force Members:

Carol Bales, OMB	Kristin Cohen, FTC[31]
Cynthia Bias, VA	Thomas Coty, DHS
Devon Bryan, IRS	John Delmore, FBI
Heidi Cross, VA	

[31] FTC staff consulted with the Task Force on privacy issues related to IdM, but did not participate in the report's formal review and clearance.

Margit Farmer, DOD

Timothy Fong, DOD

Dr. Michael Foster, NSF

Willie Graham, DOC

Dr. Myra Gray, DOD

Greg Hall, DNI

Celia Hanley, DOD

Patrick Hannon, DNI

James Hass, IC

Linda Hill, SSA

Bobby Jones, DOC

Patrick Hannon, DNI

Robert Holman, FBI

Tammy Jeske, Treasury

Deborah Lafky, HHS

Alan Lane, SSA

Naomi Lefkovitz, FTC[32]

Paul Lizotte, FAA

Adair Martinez, VA

Erika McCallister, NIST

Mark McConville, VA

William Morrison, NASA

Mary Beth Murphy, IRS

Karen Petraska, NASA

Steven Posnack, HHS

Sherry Sabol, DOJ

Peter Sand, DHS

James Schminky, Treasury

Teresa Schwarzhoff, NIST

Elizabeth Sokul, NASA

Lisa Swan, DOD

Angelika Sweitzer, IRS

Rick Therrien, IRS

Richard Thompson, DOT

Jacy Thurmond, SSA

Owen Unangst, USDA

---

[32] FTC staff consulted with the Task Force on privacy issues related to IdM, but did not participate in the report's formal review and clearance.

Annex C Presentations to the Identity Management Task Force

Date	Title	Presenter
Jan 24, 2008	Identity Management at USDA	Owen Unangst, USDA
Jan 31, 2008	Claims Will Change Everything	Kim Cameron, Micro-soft
Feb 7, 2008	Scope	Jim Dray, NIST
Feb 14, 2008	HSPD-12, Fed PKI, e-Authentication	Judith Spencer, GSA
Feb 28, 2008	Who Goes There?	Stephen Holden, CSTB, University of Md
Mar 20, 2008	Identity Mgmt Issues & Challenges	Richard Brackney, NSA
Mar 27, 2008	Identity Management	Mark Clancy, Citigroup
Apr 3, 2008	Vision of Id Management End State	William Gravell, DOD
Apr 24, 2008	Privacy Act Overview	Kristen Moncada, DOJ
May 8, 2008	REAL ID	Selden Biggs, DHS
May 22, 2008	Cyber Security	Charles Romine, OSTP

Annex D Department of Defense (DOD) Global Information Grid (GIG)

The DOD GIG is a globally interconnected, end-to-end set of information capabilities, associated processes, and personnel for collecting, processing, storing, securing, discovering, disseminating and managing information on demand to all DOD employees and contractor support personnel. Another set of users belong to family members and retirees who require access to financial and medical resources. Other potential users are federal government personnel as well as coalition and allied members.

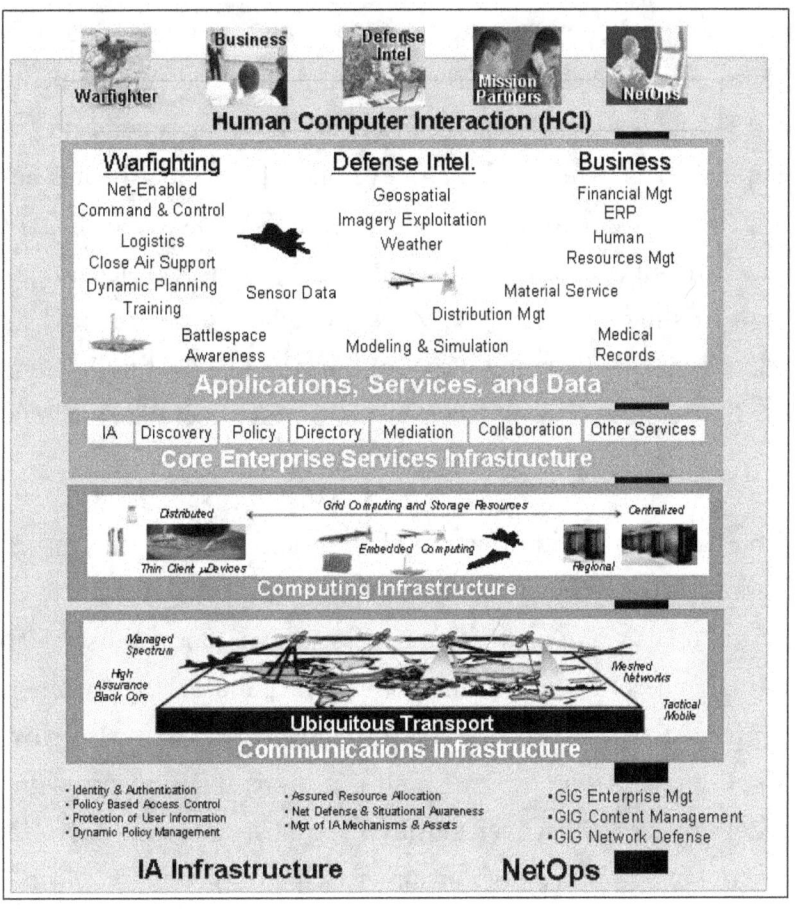

Figure D-1. The DOD Global Information Grid

As the DOD moves toward a Network-Centric operational environment with a goal of Information Superiority, it is becoming increasingly dependent on a secure and interoperable GIG. This dependence puts the Department at greater risk. The threats against DOD's Information Environment are asymmetric and the actors, methods, and tools can be very different but still have the same consequence. The threats against the people, processes and technologies can be both cyber as well as physical. A strong and resilient Identity and Privilege Management system is critical to carrying out security responsibilities.

The DOD GIG supports several domains — the DOD, National Security, and related Intelligence Community missions and business functions, in war and in peace. It provides worldwide capabilities from all operating locations to all categories of users and supports interfaces to coalition, allied, and non-DOD users and systems. There are established GIG compliance and enforcement mechanisms to achieve IT and National Security Systems (NSS) interoperability, and Information Assurance (IA). The DOD has developed IA standards and conventions in support of the GIG in coordination with the NIST. Lastly, all DOD Component-leased, -owned, -operated, or -managed GIG systems, services, upgrades, or expansions to existing systems or services are acquired or procured in compliance with the Department's Planning, Programming and Budgeting System and support a systems of systems concept capability in an interoperable, standards-based enterprise.

The demands for information sharing and a global enterprise available to users requires effective information protection measures in place to control access to authorized users while preventing access to unauthorized users. The enterprise requires trust and confidence in the identity of initiators and recipients of the requested information, and, finally, that the information is trustworthy with a high degree of certitude. At the heart of it all is a robust IdM system with its ability to collect, identify, store, discover, retrieve and share identity data securely across the DOD GIG to a multitude of consumers while protecting PII from compromise and identity theft. The DOD continues to use technology as enablers (e.g, Public Key and Biometrics) in support of IdM in order to provide higher levels of certitude about individuals, friendly, neutral or adversary, across the full range of military operations and DOD business functions.

The DOD uses Public Key (PK) technology as part of its IdM Framework. Public key cryptography is a critical element of the DOD net-centric goals in providing for identification, integrity, authenticity, confidentiality, and non-repudiation services. The public key component provides electronic credentials that are unique, un-forgeable, and trusted for use in virtual network transactions, and supports strong authentication for a broad range of human and non-person entities (devices) requesting access to DOD networks, information and resources. The PK-based authentication provides the ability to log on to network or Web-based resources, thus eliminating the inherent vulnerabilities of user ID/password/PIN. Although there are 6 million probes of DOD networks a day, successful intrusions have declined 46 percent in the past year[33] because of the requirement that all DOD personnel log on to unclassified networks using a smartcard with their PK certificate.

A PKI provides a secure infrastructure and common standards for identity proofing, credential issuance and revocation management. It is the framework and services that provide for generation, production, distribution, control, accounting and destruction of public key certificates. PKI provides IA capabilities, issuing and managing virtual identities and associated credentials and key materials for users, applications, servers, and network components. The PKI provides a foundation for interoperable security services including authentication, data integrity, and confidentiality, and also supports digital signature, access control and non-repudiation. PKI can be used to facilitate broader usage for network logon, e-mail signing, and certificate-based authentication for Web servers. PKI offers net-centric services for users to manage their credentials and for applications to authenticate certificates received during electronic transactions. It can provide the security foundation for assured information sharing across a wide range of mis-

---

[33] Lt Gen Croom, Director DISA, remarks at AFCEA SpaceComm 2007 Conference
(http://www.fcw.com/online/news/97480-1 html)

sion and business functions. The vast number of organizations beginning to use PKI makes it scalable for interactions on a global basis.

The DOD Biometrics Enterprise is an entity comprised of the Department's joint, service, and agency organizations working together to integrate biometrics into the identity transactions needed to support military operations and departmental business functions. It is a flexible, global biometrics enterprise that protects rights and enables services for friends and partners, and denies anonymity to adversaries. It is a global enterprise with accurate collection, rapid data enrollment and storage, reliable matching through multimodal fusion, real-time reach-back access, and timely reply to meet the needs of the DOD biometrics customer anytime, anywhere. The Enterprise shares biometrics data with internal, interagency, and foreign partners in accordance with law and policy. It protects biometrics data from unauthorized access, misuse, corruption, and theft and ensures that the privacy rights of U.S. citizens and allies are protected. The Enterprise also incorporates biometrics data into DOD, intelligence community, and interagency activities. A biometrics-enabled identity is used to monitor individual access privileges to DOD services and resources, or to deny a criminal or adversary the ability to hide his true identity by stripping away anonymity with swift, accurate, and definitive identity verification. Stripping away the anonymity of adversaries and verifying identities are national security interests of the highest order. The Biometrics Enterprise is a standards-based IdM service. Standardization permits access and interoperable sharing by all functional processes while, at the same time, preserving the underlying integrity of the IdM service data. Inherent in the Enterprise's ability to enhance and enable DOD business functions is the absolute assurance that the data is secure and the privacy of the Total Force and the Department's allies and partners are preserved.

Annex E Goals and Objectives for Achieving the Objective Federal IdM System

Goal #1   Deploy and Operate an IdM Framework Across the federal government

The IdM plan must realize a capability consistent with the long-term vision, which can support all entities from users to devices to systems, physical and logical access. The IdM capability must be flexible, agile, dynamic and scalable to account for and respond to the numerous changes in most organizations and mission operations. The need for higher levels of confidence in claimed identities and the safeguarding of data associated with identities of people, systems, processes and organizations underline the demand for continued IdM evolution. Enterprise services can be focused deployments, but the local entities (e.g., humans, sponsors of devices and owners of business applications) will have to be registered, issued credentials, and systems configured to use those services. This requires coordinated efforts, standards-based implementations, synchronized execution and a secure IT infrastructure to support a global, interoperable capability described below. It is acknowledged that existing activity in developing an IdM framework is underway within the federal government. The goal is to take the current activity forward by combining the different efforts being undertaken by different sectors.

Objective 1.1 Establish a Robust IdM framework for the Global Telecommunications Grid. The Global Grid supporting the IdM system must be robust — that is, it must provide adequate assurance and resilience to cyber attack to prevent compromise of the system and exploitation of the ID data. A successful IdM system will also be required to support a wide variety of privacy and security levels, ranging from low-security password-based single-factor authentication to high-end attribute-based systems employing state of the art privacy-enhancing techniques. Technical aspects of this problem can be addressed conceptually by designing an appropriate IdM framework.

The IdM framework should:

- Associate people and devices with an identity (PKI, biometric, other). This identity will be used to access facilities and networks;

- Use shared standards, protocols and infrastructure to support both logical and physical access to resources;

- Use a federated approach. It will recognize approved credentials from industry, government and foreign partners;

- Marry identity information with attributes associated with an entity to facilitate access to facilities and resources;

- Create authoritative sources to house and maintain attribute-related information on people and devices.

-

Goal #2   Leverage the Success of Ongoing IdM Investments

Many agencies in the federal government have made significant progress in the deployment and operation of IdM capabilities. These investments require full life cycle support, and, in many cases, have to incorporate enhancements (e.g., extended support for security and interoperability with an expanded set of external partners) to retain their utility.

Objective 2.1. Execute Ongoing IdM Programs — There are several key programs and initiatives among the different agencies that represent significant investment and have to be leveraged. Each focuses on a specific aspect of IdM (e.g., PIV Card, PKI, identity issuance, biometrics, and attributes) and delivers operational capabilities that are integral to a comprehensive and secure IdM service within their respective agencies. They can provide identity determinations to higher levels of certainty. These activities must continue to be funded and executed.

Objective 2.2. Align and Execute IdM Initiatives — Since these initiatives have many complex interrelationships, it may be necessary to identify and implement adjustments that ensure technical integration and alignment to deliver true operational improvements while providing for interoperability across the agencies.

Goal #3   Implement Additional IdM Initiatives

The evolution of IdM has to extend capabilities beyond those addressed in ongoing investments. As with the ongoing efforts, these have to be planned and executed to enable integration and synchronization.

Objective 3.1. Develop an Overarching IdM Framework — Any implementation this broad in scale and magnitude will have to be implemented over time to leverage various technologies and user circumstances. To ensure that the evolution leads to the desired result, the federal government will have to establish and ratify a technical framework that defines the functionality, performance, interfaces, and associated standards and specifications needed to guide each initiative.

Objective 3.2. Implement Additional IdM Capabilities — Since there will be additional capabilities that may be needed to reach the IdM vision, it will be necessary to find a means for their implementation. These could be structured as enhanced functionality within ongoing programs or as new initiatives. In either case, these capabilities will have to be engineered and integrated into the broader IdM fabric.

Objective 3.3. HSPD-12/FIPS 201-1. — With the issuance of Homeland Security Presidential Directive 12 (HSPD-12) and the subsequent release of FIPS 201-1 by NIST, there was a significant move away from the silo approach toward interoperability. FIPS 201-1 mandates common standards for the identity proofing of all federal employees and all contractors working for the federal government.

The mandated standards of the PIV card systems and the use of newer technologies in their development has created an opportunity to build on the new systems. Within the federal government, the PIV card is a new opportunity that should be leveraged as the basis for enhanced functionality and can be used as a model for the development of other systems that need to share data across agencies.

Goal #4   Federate IdM to Enable Operations with Partners

The IdM framework must consider the concept of External Access Points that will provide the connection and the functions necessary for two federated enterprises to support transactions across the interface. Each agency in the federal government operations will rely on collaboration and knowledge sharing with other agencies to include the intelligence community, state/local/tribal governments, industry, allies and coalition partners, and foreign governments in order to conduct business. This demands a trust framework among the various players and an IdM capability to support this scope of interoperation. It must also be noted that by nature of their missions, some federal agencies must be able to selectively interoperate, allowing some access to systems and data while denying that access to others. Future federations must acknowledge and incorporate the trust framework into their solutions.

Objective 4.1 Enhance the Emerging IdM Federation. — A federation is a collection of organizations, requiring a formal governance structure to be established, with each member agreeing to adhere to a set of standards and policies that enable the execution and operation of a common IdM system within each organization. A secure and interoperable IdM system is an important objective for the federal government, as identity credentials must cross agency networks, as well as their applications. Through the use of electronic identity credentials, organizations can establish trust relationships among the agencies' unique IdM systems. To accomplish this objective, the IdM Federation must leverage identity credentials across multiple trust environments and enable identity assurance services for federal electronic business processes, which will enable trust and confidence in government transactions through the establishment of an integrated policy and technical infrastructure for identity management. Governance and compliance with assurance level policy, technical standards for connectivity, content and security management will be critical to solving the technical interoperability challenges.

From the perspective of users and operators, an envisioned IdM Federation will operate seamlessly and transparently with its counterparts in external partner environments. Operations with these partners will be driven by policies, supported by operational procedures, and safeguarded with technical enforcement mechanisms to control the ability to interact with them and allow access to resources. In addition to policies, there are legal and regulatory restrictions on various aspects of IdM functionality.

Objective 4.2. Develop Federation Guidelines — While implementations are focused on the use of commercial standards, extending operations requires a strategy that allows each member organization the prerogative to control its own implementation and still enable a means for interoperation. From the perspective of users, the envisioned IdM Federation will operate seamlessly and transparently in external partner environments.

Goal #5   Align IdM Governance, Policy and Guidance

Every federal government department and agency has an expansive set of written policies concerning identity management and access control. Over time, a divergence has materialized due to the local development of procedures and the differing interpretations of the various organizations. As a result, agencies are recognizing the importance of having comprehensive, community-wide policies that can be implemented with a common set of procedures across the IdM enterprise. The IA and IdM policies currently in use should be reviewed, with the goal of refreshing and aligning them to ensure consistency as the next generation IdM framework is developed. Governance of this activity rests with the Federal CIO Council, comprised of the Chief Information Officers of all cabinet-level departments and other independent agencies.

Annex F Roadmap for Developing the Standards in Global Standards Organizations that are Necessary to Achieve a Global IdM system

This annex elaborates on the work that needs to be done in the standards development area in order to achieve the vision of the global IdM framework that is described in the main body of this report, of which the federal IdM would be an integral component.

In order to achieve a global IdM system, global standards will need to be developed with respect to the three major functions performed: management, bridging, and identity.

The federal government needs to be involved in these standardization processes in order to ensure that the global standards that are developed can support federal requirements (e.g., for priority communications in emergency situations) and policies (e.g., privacy policies).

Objective 1. Develop global standards for managing an IDM framework — The management function of a successful IDM framework addresses the crucial functions of secure life cycle maintenance of data as identities are established, proofed, modified, suspended, terminated, archived, or reallocated. In order for a global IdM system t be successful the requirements and processes for each of these life cycle events must be agreed by all participants in the global community. The ability to trust globally is directly impacted by the confidence each participating IdM places in the life cycle management of the others. Three models of the management function have been identified, depending on whether the identity data is controlled by a network (the network-centric model), a user (the user-centric model, where the users have a role to play in managing the data about them that resides in a data source), or a service provider (the service-centric model). The management function for each identity management system includes access control mechanisms such as authentication, authorization, and auditing of managers and users as well as possible user certification by a third party for that individual IdM system or federation of systems. Security assurance is part of the access control mechanism.

The management function for an IdM system is depicted within the blue boxes in Figure F-1 below. These boxes represent different IdM systems or federations of systems. A party (the "relying party") within System A wants to validate the identity of some entity with whom the relying party wants to enter into a transaction. The relying party seeks to validate the identity of that entity by requesting assistance from an identity provider. The identity provider may be able to find the identity information within System A, in which case it needs to pass through an access control process to establish it meets the requisite security profile and is entitled to obtain the data from the data repository. (If the identity information is not in System A, the information provider will have to "discover" the necessary identity information by going outside System A, using a bridging function involving a data model to find some other IdM system (System B) that has the requisite information and communicate with it.)

The data model acts as a trusted technical intermediary; it can map or translate all relevant identity data structures into a common data structure.

Objective 2. Develop global standards for the bridging function of an IDM framework. The objective of the bridging function in an IdM framework is to bridge the differences between disparate identity management systems or federations of systems. To be successful, a bridging function must enable a wide variety of requests for identity information to be mapped against a wide variety of identity data repositories across different trust domains.[34] A successful IDM framework must be sufficiently flexible and technologically neutral to support

----

[34] A trust domain is the area defined by the boundaries of a federation, where all elements are under the control of owners who have defined the limits and mechanisms for achieving trust and have agreed to implement them. A trust domain in the IdM context would consist of those identity providers, relying parties, and perhaps end-users who have already agreed to a collection of usage and maintenance policies.

different situations and types of identity management infrastructures, and to support the multitude of existing and emerging identity management systems.

The bridging function of an IdM framework is depicted in Figure F-1. The figure shows two IdM systems (or federations of systems) that are unrelated to each other and do not share the same data formats. In this case, a **data requestor** (an identity provider) in System A, upon discovering that desired identity data resides in a data source in some System B with which it has no relationship, sends the request through a **bridge** involving an identity data model. At the front end of the bridge is the relevant access profile that authenticates the requestor and applies security and other policies to authorize the transaction. The access profile translates the request into the universal standard language of the data model, understood by all profiles, and forwards the request to the relevant data profile, which translates it from the globally standardized language of the data model to a format that the discovered **data source** can understand. The data source provides the required data, following the same process in reverse. This two-step translation process simplifies the translation capability set required by any single profile.

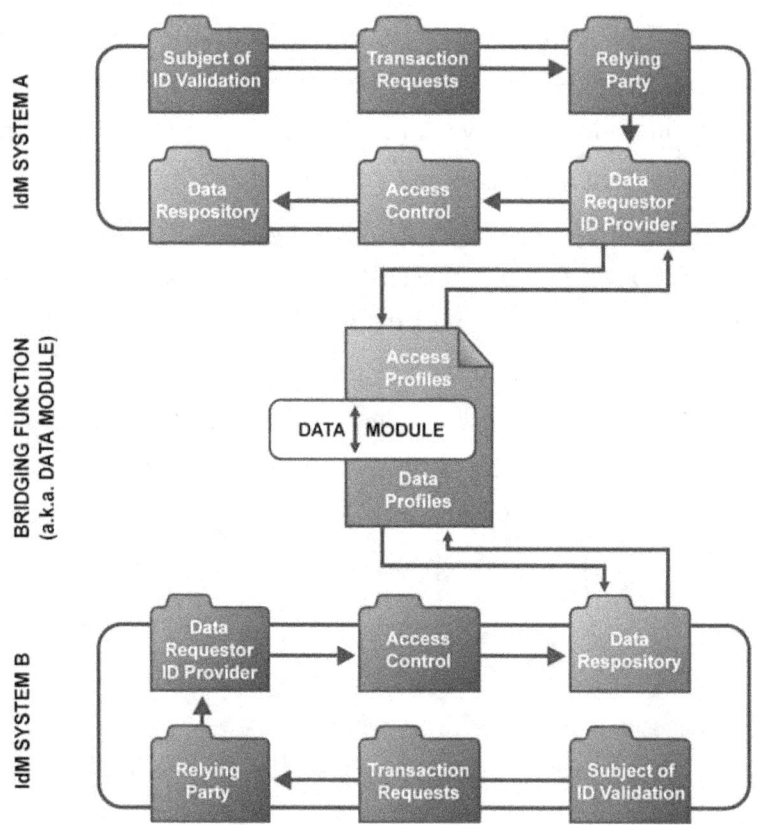

Figure F-1. The Bridging and Management Functions in an IdM framework

Objective 3. Develop global standards for the identity function of an IDM framework. — The third major aspect of the IdM framework is the identity function. In contrast to the bridging function, which addresses interworking horizontally across different systems and federations of systems, the identity function addresses vertical consistency between the identity data used in the different network application, service and transport levels. Standards need to be developed to serve the identity needs all three stratums consistently.

Objective 4. Develop federal requirements and policies that the U.S. wants to have reflected in the development of global standards. — The design of specific standards for the IDM framework will depend heavily on the requirements and policies that it must meet. The federal government has an important role to play in identifying the requirements and policies that global technical standards need to support.

Policies and requirements determine how trust is defined and established (e.g., what information will be revealed, to which parties, for which purposes, and how it is to be treated). Standards development organizations do not develop policies and requirements. However, standards-setting bodies must develop technical solutions that can accommodate the entire range of non-technical policies and requirements that governments and businesses develop. Governments and regional groups establish some policies and requirements, such as for privacy and compliance. Businesses establish other policies and requirements, such as for the protection of proprietary information and quality control. Within these categories (businesses and governments), different identity management systems may operate under different policies.

In developing policies for identity management systems, a balance needs to be struck between the need to control access and the need for users to be able to obtain access as rapidly, transparently and seamlessly as possible. Policies and requirements should not be needlessly complex or expensive to implement.

Policies also govern the issuance of identities. hey establish what constitutes a sufficiently unambiguous representation of an entity for the intended context or application and travel with the identity information throughout its lifetime to ensure that the information is indeed used only in accord with the policy (e.g., for the purposes to which the user consented). PII requires special protection. This may include, among other things, that Identity Providers attach enforceable policies to PII, provide for the confidentiality and integrity of PII, and minimize the amount of PII used by applications. Equipment standards need to reflect these capabilities and requirements.

Annex G Data Call Instruments and Results

Many questions were initially posited by the Task Force:

1. How many government programs contain Personally Identifiable Information (PII)?
2. How prevalent is the application of biometric technologies?
3. Do agencies rely on internally or externally generated digital identities?
4. What challenges are agencies facing with respect to IdM?
5. What mechanisms exist to provide insight into the state of practice for IdM in federal government programs?

In order to help answer these questions, the Task Force conducted two analyses:

1. A data call was conducted across many federal agency Chief Information Officers (CIOs) in order to provide a simple, first-order understanding of digital IdM application and issues. This Annex provides the results of this data call.
2. A large number of Privacy Impact Assessments (PIAs) were collected and analyzed in order to quickly and easily gain insight into how widespread a range of technologies has been implemented in government programs. Most, but not all, of the technologies analyzed were related to the application of biometrics. The subsequent Annex provides the results of the PIA assessment.

To ensure that the Task Force final report could be broadly disseminated, sensitive and classified information was not requested.

In order to obtain a simple, first-order understanding of digital IdM application and issues, the Task Force conducted a survey of information systems across the Federal Executive Branch. In coordination with the Office of Management and Budget (OMB), and through the Chief Information Officer (CIO) Council, the 28 agency CIOs of the CIO Council were asked to provide information the following topics:

1. For each information system that the agency includes in their regular FISMA reports,[35] describe:
   a. The number of systems that contain federal information in identifiable form.
   b. The type of information being collected (e.g., PIN/password, date of birth, Social Security number (SSN), fingerprint).
   c. The number of systems that use digital IDs generated externally from the agency.
   d. The number of systems that request information from external parties to establish a digital ID.
   e. The number of systems that fall under a set of particular sectors.
2. Each agency was also asked to provide information on the following:
   a. List and describe the major IdM initiatives within the agency.
   b. List the agency's top three IdM priorities.
   c. List the agency's top three IdM challenges.
   d. List any agency-developed IdM "use cases."
   e. List and describe the IdM collaborative efforts your agency participates in (both interagency and industry efforts).
   f. List the agency's biggest in addressing privacy concerns related to IdM systems.
   g. Discuss whether the agency has developed any policies or procedures related to addressing privacy concerns raised by IdM systems.
3. Each agency was also asked to provide information on the following:
   a. Discuss whether the agency is funding any science and technology research efforts in the area of IdM.
   b. Discuss whether the agency is participating in any IdM related standards activities.
4. Each agency was also asked to provide recommendations to the Task Force.

Agencies were provided with a copy of the Task Force charter, a list of Task Force participants, instructions for filling out the questionnaire and the data call questionnaire instrument. This annex provides the Task Force's IdM questionnaire and the summary results of the responses received. The results are interspersed with the questionnaire that was distributed. Text that has a box around it is

---

[35]In support of reporting requirements established by the Federal Information Security Management Act of 2002, the Office of Management and Budget (OMB) regularly requires agencies to report on several metrics that relate to information privacy.

from the questionnaire; text without a box represents high-level summary observations. Many agencies reported data at the component or bureau level, but the data has been "rolled up" and is presented at the agency level. Some text has also been redacted to remove references to agency names and initiatives. Raw data collected is included at the end of this annex.

April 17, 2008

MEMORANDUM FOR CIO COUNCIL

FROM: Jim Dray (NIST), Judith Spencer (GSA) and Duane Blackburn (OSTP)
           NSTC Task Force on IdM Co-Chairs

VIA: Carol Bales
           Office of Management and Budget

SUBJECT: NSTC Task Force Inventory of Federal Identity Management Systems

The National Science and Technology Council (NSTC) Task Force on Identity Management (IdM) is requesting your assistance as we study existing IdM activities in the US Government. This interagency Task Force was established to assess the status of and challenges related to IdM technologies, and develop recommendations regarding Federal government's science and technology needs in this area. The work of the Task Force is envisioned as a starting point, and foundation, for future government coordination activities in IdM. A copy of the charter and list of participants is attached for your reference.

One of the assigned tasks of the Task Force is to establish a current baseline of activities, applications, and challenges. The Task Force plans to approach this task in multiple ways, one of which is to request assistance from agency CIO offices to inventory ongoing and upcoming Federal IdM programs. We respectfully request your support by completing the attached survey, which was modeled after FISMA reporting that you have recently completed in order to minimize effort on your part. The results of this inventory will be included in the Task Force's final report.

For the purposes of this Task Force, "identity management" is defined as "the combination of technical systems, rules and procedures that define the ownership, utilization, and safeguard of personal identity information. The primary goal of the Identity Management process is to assign attributes to a digital identity, and to connect that identity to an individual."

Please send an electronic copy of the completed survey to bbrykczynski@ostp.eop.gov by May 9, 2008. You may contact Duane Blackburn, dblackburn@ostp.eop.gov, for general questions about the Task Force and Bill Brykczynski, bbrykczynski@ostp.eop.gov for technical questions about this survey.

The Task Force thanks you in advance for your assistance.

Attachments
  • Instructions for Completing the Inventory Template
  • IdM Inventory Template
  • Task Force Charter
  • Task Force Membership

Instructions for Completing the Inventory

Each of the worksheets in the attached inventory template are to be completed by the appropriate agency officials, as part of one combined report, and transmitted electronically to Bill Brykczynski (bbrykczynski@ostp.eop.gov) by May 9, 2008. All parts of the report should be transmitted in the contents of one single e-mail. No additional transmittal letter is required.

The remaining sections contain additional definitions and instructions clarifying the types of information being requested in this inventory.

GENERAL TERMS

The following terms are used throughout the document.

Identity – the unique biological person defined by DNA; the physical being

Digital Identity (Digital ID) – the representation of Identity in a digital environment.

User – the individual whose identity or digital identity must be verified. In e-government applications the user may be a citizen interacting directly with the system. In law enforcement or border crossing applications the "user" may be a third party whose asserted identity is being checked against a watchlist by a law enforcement officer.

QUESTION 1

Question 1a

This inventory builds on data reported by your agency in compliance with the Federal Information Security Management Act (FISMA). Please ensure that the totals in question 1a of this inventory match what your agency most recently reported to OMB in M07-19 Section D – Senior Agency Official for Privacy (SAOP) Question 1a. Otherwise, please provide an explanation in the Comments section. Answers to 1b-1e should be new data.

Eighteen member organizations of the CIO Council representing fifteen departments or agencies provided responses. In addition, three small agencies also provided survey responses. Thus, a total of eighteen departments or agencies provided survey responses. The responses covered approximately 191 agency components or bureaus and described a total of 3,400 information technology programs or systems. Just over half of the programs and systems in the response were from the Department of Defense (DOD). Table G-1 below provides a summary of the number of systems by agency represented in the data call response. Note that the Department of Energy (DoE) provided a response to the data call but did not answer the system specific questions; thus, no systems are reported in Table G-1 from DoE.

Agency	Total	Percentage
DHS	111	3.3%
DOC	46	1.4%
DOD	1,888	55.5%
DoE	0	0.0%
DoI	152	4.5%
DOJ	152	4.5%
DOS	91	2.7%
EPA	35	1.0%
GSA	83	2.4%
HUD	75	2.2%
NARA	36	1.1%
NASA	57	1.7%
NRC	38	1.1%
RRB	21	0.6%
SSA	20	0.6%
SSS	3	0.1%
Treasury	404	11.9%
USDA	188	5.5%
Grand Total	**3,400**	**100.0%**

Table G-1. Summary of Total Systems

Question 1.b: Provide a count of the number of systems (that are regularly reported on in FISMA report to OMB) for which the following information are:

Login Alias — a string selected by the user or assigned by the system that does not necessarily reflect the user's legal name. Common examples are an email address, account number, or screen name.

PIN/Password — a string used in conjunction with another identifier, such as a login alias, that the user inputs when requesting authentication.

Legal Name — a name associated with the identity of a real person through identity proofing

DOB — date of Birth.

SSN — Social Security number.

Fingerprint(s) — one or more digitized fingerprint images suitable for matching to the user's fingers.

Iris — images of the irises of one or both of the user's eyes suitable for iris recognition.

Facial Image — images of a face or head suitable for either human or electronic facial recognition.

Other Biometric — Iin the Comments section below questions 1a-f, please list any additional biometric data collected and used by the system.

Security Question(s) — questions such as, "What is your mother's maiden name?" or, "What is your favorite color?" to which the user must supply a pre-stored answer.

Token — hardware or software token issued to the user. Includes RSA SecurID tokens and keys stored on HSPD-12 Smart Cards.

> **Other (List)** — in the Comments section below questions 1a-f, please list any additional identification information collected and used by the system.

The most common forms of information being collected for IdM are login alias, PIN/password, legal name, date of birth and Social Security number. Interestingly, more than 27 percent of the all systems store Social Security numbers.

Few systems or programs collect or use biometric-related data (e.g., fingerprints, iris or facial imaging) or use security questions or tokens. See Table G-2 for a summary of the results of this portion of the data call. Note that many systems collect more than one of the identified information elements (e.g., a system may collect both a Social Security number and a PIN/password), so the percentages do not sum to 100 percent.

Type of Information	Total No. of Systems	Percentage (N/3400)
Login Alias	798	23.5%
PIN/Password	1573	46.3%
Legal Name	906	26.6%
Date of Birth	450	13.2%
Social Security Number	930	27.4%
Fingerprint(s)	76	2.2%
Iris	7	0.2%
Facial Image	59	1.7%
Other Biometric (List)	15	0.4%
Security Question(s)	29	0.9%
Token	308	9.1%
Other (List)	91	2.7%
Grand Total	**5242**	

Table G-2. Number of Systems for Which the Following Information

Is Collected

> **Question 1.c: Provide a count of the number of systems that use digital IDs generated externally from the Agency. Please describe in Comments section.** An externally generated digital ID is a digital ID (see above) that is not created or managed by your agency. In Question 1c, indicate the number of systems that do not maintain their own authentication systems, but, instead, trust the digital ID verified by a system external to your agency.

Although agencies identified 28 systems that used externally generated digital IDs, only a few were mentioned in the comments section. Those that were mentioned included Verisign external digital certificates, DOD Common Access Cards (CAC), GSA's Federal E-Authentication Federation project, the Federal Bridge Certificate Authority, a Department of Treasury application that generates certificates and another agency system that generates certificates for an electronic hearing docket system.

> **Question 1.d: Provide a count of the number of systems that request information from external parties to establish a digital ID. Please describe in Comments section.** Indicate the number of systems that request information from identity systems outside your agency when establishing a digital ID. Examples include verifying legal name-SSN combinations with the Social Security Administration or retrieving a name based on biometric data stored by the FBI.

Examples of such systems provided to the agency included verifying legal name-Social Security number combinations with the Social Security Administration or retrieving a name based on biometric data stored by the FBI. Agencies identified 28 systems that request information from external parties to establish a digital ID, but few were specifically mentioned in the comments section.

Agency Name

1. Inventory of Systems that Contain Federal Information in Identifiable Form

1. In the table below, identify the total number of agency information systems by component/bureau. Extend the worksheet onto subsequent pages if necessary to include all Component/Bureaus.

For this inventory, agency systems include information systems used or operated by the agency or by a contractor on behalf of the Agency. Please ensure that the totals in question 1a of this inventory match what the agency reported to OMB in Section D (SAOP) Question 1a of your agency's most recent Agency's Federal Information Security Management Act (FISMA) submission. Otherwise, please provide an explanation in the Comments section.

In column (a) of the table below, identify by component/bureau the number of Agency information systems that contain Federal information in identifiable form. In column (b), identify the number of systems in (a) for which the listed identifiable information is collected. Each system in (a) may have multiple entries in column (b). In column (c), identify the number of systems in (a) which rely on externally generated digital ID. In column (d), indicate the number of systems that provide information in response to requests from outside the Agency. Descriptions and explanations can be written in the Comments section below the table.

	a.	b.												c.	d.
	Number of systems that contain Federal information in identifiable form	Number of systems in (a) for which the following information are collected												Number of systems in (a) that use digital IDs generated externally from the Agency. Please describe in Comments section.	Number of systems in (a) that request information from external parties to establish a digital ID. Please describe in Comments section.
Component/Bureau	Total Systems	Login Alias	PIN / Password	Legal Name	DOB	SSN	Fingerprint(s)	Iris	Facial Image	Other Biometric (List)	Security Question(s)	Token	Other (List)	Total Systems	Total Systems
Example Component/Bureau	100													80	80
Agency Totals	0	0	0	0	0	0	0	0	0	0	0	0	0	0	0

Comments

Question 1.e: Provide a count of the number of systems that fall under the listed sectors.

The columns labeled "Component/Bureau" and "a." will be automatically filled based on the data you provided for questions 1a-d. They are reprinted on this sheet for reference purposes.

Sectors

Personnel Mgmt –

Financial Mgmt –

Acquisition –

Healthcare

Entitlement payments –

Tax collection –

Licensing –

Passport/Visa –

Border-crossing security –

Military –

Intelligence –

Cybersecurity –

Law enforcement –

Physical Access –

Logical/network Access –

Retail e-commerce –

Telebanking –

NSTC Task Force on Identity Management Inventory of Federal Systems: Question 1e

Agency Name

1. Inventory of Systems that Contain Federal Information in Identifiable Form

1. In the table below, identify the systems in (a) by service sector. Choose the sector that best fits.

Component/Bureau	a. Number of systems that contain Federal information in identifiable form — Agency Systems	e. Number of systems in (a) that fall under the following sectors																
		Government Operations			Citizen Services				Security							Access Controls		Web-based Processes	
		Personnel Mgmnt	Financial Mgmnt	Acquisition	Healthcare	Entitlement payments	Tax collection	Licensing	Passport/visa	Border-crossing security	Military	Intelligence	Cybersecurity	Law enforcement	Physical	Logical/network	Retail e-commerce	Telebanking
Example Component/Bureau	100																	
0	0																	
0	0																	
0	0																	
0	0																	
0	0																	
0	0																	
0	0																	
0	0																	
0	0																	
0	0																	
0	0																	
0	0																	
0	0																	
0	0																	
0	0																	
0	0																	
0	0																	
0	0																	
0	0																	
0	0																	
0	0																	
0	0																	
Agency Totals	0	0	0	0	0	0	0	0	0	0	0	0	0	0	0	0	0	0

Comments

Table G-3 rolls up the count and percentages of systems within each sector. The majority of the systems reported on in this data call were financial management systems.

		Government Operations			Citizen Services					Security					Access Controls		Web-based Processes	
		Personnel Mgmt	Financial Mgmt	Acquisition	Healthcare	Entitlement Payments	Tax Collection	Licensing	Passport/Visa	Border-crossing Security	Military	Intelligence	Cyber security	Law Enforcement	Physical	Logical/Network	Retail e-commerce	Telebanking
Count		333	807	60	21	74	153	25	40	15	2	20	7	111	46	203	11	73
Percentage		16.6%	40.3%	3.0%	1.0%	3.7%	7.6%	1.2%	2.0%	0.7%	0.1%	1.0%	0.3%	5.5%	2.3%	10.1%	0.5%	3.6%

Table G-3. Number of Systems per Sector

QUESTION 2

No additional instructions. See the inventory template.

	NSTC Task Force on Identity Management Inventory of Federal Systems: Question 2	
Agency Name:		
	2. Identity Management Initiatives and Privacy Concerns	
2a.	List and descr be the major identity management initiatives within your agency.	
2b.	What are the agency's top three identity management priorities?	
2c.	What major identity management challenges does your agency face?	
2d.	Has your organization developed any "use cases" with respect to identity management? If so, may the Task Force have access to them? Please descr be. (e.g., CONOPS documents)	
2e.	List and descr be the identity management collaborative efforts your organization participates in. Include both interagency and industry efforts.	
2f.	What are the biggest challenges you face in addressing privacy concerns related to identity management systems?	
2g.	Have you developed any policies or procedures related to addressing privacy concerns raised by identity management systems?	

> **Question 2.a: List and describe the major IdM initiatives within your agency.**

Seventeen of the 18 responding departments or agencies reported major initiatives directly related to HSPD-12 and PIV cards. Two departments, DOD and Treasury, reported major initiatives involving SSN reduction efforts.

> **Question 2.b: What are the agency's top three IdM priorities?**

Twelve of the 18 responding departments or agencies reported top management priorities directly related to HSPD-12 and PIV cards. Several agencies also described single sign-on, centralized agency IdM, encryption, and two-factor authentication as top agency priorities.

> **Question 2.c: What major IdM challenges does your agency face?**

Eight of the 18 responding departments or agencies reported top management priorities directly related to HSPD-12 and PIV cards. Seven of the responding departments or agencies reported identity-related priorities associated with interfacing with state, local, tribal, or foreign partners.

> **Question 2.d: Has your organization developed any "use cases" with respect to IdM? If so, may the Task Force have access to them? Please describe. (e.g., CONOPS documents).**

Eight respondents representing 5 departments or agencies reported developing use cases or concept of operations (CONOPS) documents. These use cases or CONOPS documents generally are related to HSPD-12 implementation, E-Authentication, and PKI implementation.

> **Question 2.e: List and describe the IdM collaborative efforts your organization participates in. Include both interagency and industry efforts.**

Over two dozen IdM related efforts were identified by respondents. These efforts include internal-agency, interagency, industry, and standards activities. They include:

a. DOD Biometrics Task Force (BTF)
b. Attribute Based Access Control Working Group (ABACWG)
c. Biometrics Security Consortium
d. Biometrics Coordination Group
e. Committee on National Security Systems
f. Cyber Security Sub Council
g. DMDC Working groups
h. Defense Enrollment Eligibility Reporting System
i. Defense Science Board Task Force on Defense Biometrics
j. DOD Identity Protection and Management Senior Coordinating Group (IPMSCG)
k. DOD PKI Certificate Policy Management Working Group (CPMWG)
l. E-Authentication E-Gov initiative
m. Evaluation Program Technical Working Group (EPTWG)
n. Federal Identity Credential Committee (FICC)
o. Federal PKI Policy Authority
p. Federated ID management pilot with the Directorate of National Intelligence
q. FISMA initiative
r. Government Smart Card Interagency Advisory Board
s. GSA E-Authentication Technical Working Group
t. GSA HSPD-12 architecture working group (AWG)
u. GSA PKI Working Group
v. HSPD-12
w. ISC (Interagency Security Committee)
x. ISO/IEC SC 37 (Biometrics)
y. ISO/IEC/JTC1/SC27 (IT Security Techniques)
z. NCITS M1 (Biometrics)
aa. NSTC Subcommittee on Biometrics and IdM
bb. OASIS
cc. Security Industry Alliance (SIA)
dd. SmartCard Alliance (SCA)
ee. SmartCard IAB (Industry Advisory Board)
ff. SSN Tiger Team (a federal government collaborative effort to determine a solution for eliminating the use of SSNs)
gg. Treasury Privacy Committee

Question 2.f: What are the biggest challenges you face in addressing privacy concerns related to IdM systems?

Many respondents cited funding challenges associated with addressing privacy concerns. A few concerns to highlight include:

- Expanding information sharing in the information sharing environment while simultaneously safeguarding personally identifiable information.

- Rapid technology proliferation is outpacing policy implementation.

- Consistent application of policy guidelines throughout the enterprise.

- While security and privacy usually work well together, with often overlapping goals, IdM is one area where security needs and the rights to privacy can come into conflict.

- Lack of globally unique identifiers.

Question 2.g: Have you developed any policies or procedures related to addressing privacy concerns raised by IdM systems?

Of those departments or agencies describing privacy-related policies or procedures, most involved the requirements (agency-specific or otherwise) to develop PIAs or System of Records Notices (SORNs). Several agencies reported other privacy-related policies and procedures that were not specifically related to PIAs and SORNs. Eight of the 16 responding departments or agencies reported internal agency policies or procedures relating to privacy topics.

Question 2.h: Is your agency funding any science and technology research efforts in the area of IdM? If so, please describe.

Only the DOJ and DOD reported funding IdM science and technology research. The FBI listed two efforts: FBI Biometrics Center of Excellence and the CJIS Next Generation Identification. The DOD listed the Primary Staff Assistant for biometrics, and the Director of Defense Biometrics.

QUESTION 3

No additional instructions. See the inventory template.

NSTC Task Force on Identity Management Inventory of Federal Systems: Question 3				
Agency Name				
3. Research and Standards				

3.a. Is your agency funding any science and technology research efforts in the area of identity management? If so, please describe.

3.b. Is your agency involved in any of the following Federal, national, international, or industry-related standards activities? Please only list those that are related to identity management.

Enter 1 to the left of each standards organization your agency has participated in.
Only include those that are related to identity management.

Activity	Point of Contact (POC)			
	Title/Role	Name	Phone	Email
ITU-T Focus Group on Identity Management				
ITU-T Study Group 13 (Next Generation Networks)				
ITU-T Study Group 17 (Security, Languages and Telecommunication Security)				
ITU-T Other (related to identity management)				
ISO/ EC/JTC1/SC27 (IT Security Techniques)				
ISO/ EC SC 27 (Biometrics)				
ISO Other (related to identity management)				
3rd Generation Partnership Project (3GPP)				
Alliance for Telecommunications Industry Solutions (ATIS)				
European Telecommunications Standards Institute (ETSI)				
Initiative for Open Authentication (OATH)				
Internet Engineering Task Force (ETF)				
Liberty Alliance Project				
Open Mobile Alliance (OMA)				
Organization for Economic Cooperation and Development (OECD)				
Organization for the Advancement of Structured Information Standards (OASIS)				
World Wide Web Consortium (W3C)				
Other (Please list below)				

Question 3.a: Is your agency involved in any of the following federal, national, international, or industry-related standards activities? Please only list those that are related to IdM. Provide the position, name, and contact information of any agency employees who attend meetings or contribute to the deliberations of the following standards activities on behalf of your agency or component/bureau. At the end of the table, please list any additional IdM-related standard setting activities your agency participates in.

ITU-T — International Telecommunication Union — Telecommunication Standardization Bureau.

ITU-T Study Group 13 (Next Generation Networks)

ITU-T Study Group 17 (Security, Languages and Telecommunication Security)

ISO — International Organization for Standardization.

IETF — Internet Engineering Task Force

W3C — World Wide Web Consortium

OASIS — Organization for the Advancement of Structured Information Standards

OECD — Organization for Economic Co-operation and Development

ETSI — European Telecommunications Standards Institute

Liberty Alliance Project — A business alliance, formed in September 2001 with the goal of establishing an open standard for federated IdM.

3GPP — 3rd Generation Partnership Project

ATIS — Alliance for Telecommunications Industry Solutions

OMA — Open Mobile Alliance

OATH — Initiative for Open Authentication

Table G-4 provides a list of agencies that reported having participants in 14 different standards-related activities.

Activity	Participating Agency
ITU-T Study Group 13 (Next Generation Networks)	DOS
ITU-T Study Group 17 (Security, Languages and Telecommunication Security)	DOS
ITU-T Other (related to identity management)	*None Identified*
ISO/IEC/JTC1/SC27 (IT Security Techniques)	GSA and DOD
ISO/IEC/JTC1/SC37 (Biometrics)	GSA and DOD
ISO Other (related to identity management)	*None Identified*
3rd Generation Partnership Project (3GPP)	*None Identified*
Alliance for Telecommunications Industry Solutions (ATIS)	*None Identified*
European Telecommunications Standards Institute (ETSI)	*None Identified*
Initiative for Open Authentication (OATH)	NASA
Internet Engineering Task Force (IETF)	NASA
Liberty Alliance Project	GSA and NASA
Open Mobile Alliance (OMA)	*None Identified*
Organization for Economic Cooperation and Development (OECD)	DOS
Organization for the Advancement of Structured Information Standards (OASIS)	GSA and DOD
World Wide Web Consortium (W3C)	*None Identified*
Other (Please list below)	*None Identified*
INCITS M1 (Biometrics)	DOD
The Open Group	NASA
Overall NIST IdM Activities Contact	DOC
OAS CITEL PCC.I	DOS
APEC TEL	DOS

Table G-4. Agencies Participating on IdM Standards Activities

> **Question 3.b: Do you have any recommendations for the Task Force?**

Several agencies provided recommendations to the Task Force. Some of the recommendations included the following:

- Explore the use of an alternate identifier vice use of the SSN.
- Standardize IdM requirements and fund IdM initiatives.
- Designate OPM as the authoritative source of Person Identifiers across the entire federal government.

QUESTION 4

Use the box below question 4 to provide feedback on the inventory or provide any additional information you think will help the Task Force assess the status of and challenges related to IdM technologies, and develop recommendations regarding the federal government's science and technology needs in this area.

QUESTION 5

No additional instructions. See the inventory template.

NSTC Task Force on Identity Management Inventory of Federal Systems: Questions 4 and 5			
Agency Name:			
4. Additional Comments and Recommendations			
Do you have any recommendations for the Task Force?			
5. Identity Management Points of Contact Information			
If the Task Force has follow-up questions, please provide the names and contact information for one to three identity management technical experts within your agency.			
Title/Role (e.g., CIO, SAOP, other)	**Name**	**Phone**	**E-mail**

4.4.1.1.1.G.1   Data Call Results. Question 1b: Provide a Count of the Number of Systems

| | 1a Total Systems | 1b Number of systems in (a) for which the following information are collected | | | | | | | | | | | | 1c Total Systems | 1d Total Systems | 1e Number of systems in (a) that fall under the following sectors | | | | | | | | | | | | | | | | |
Agency	Total Systems	Login Alias	PIN/Password	Legal Name	DOB	SSN	Fingerprint(s)	Iris	Facial Image	Other Biometric (List)	Security Question(s)	Token	Other (List)	(uses external digital IDs)	(requests info to establish digital ID)	Personnel Mgmt	Financial Mgmt	Acquisition	Healthcare	Entitlement payments	Tax collection	Licensing	Passport/visa	Border-crossing security	Military	Intelligence	Cybersecurity	Law enforcement	Physical	Logical/network	Retail e-commerce	Telebanking
DHS	111	24	23	71	53	31	50	6	36	12	3	12	38	1	9	20	6	1	1	1		2	3	12		9	2	36	13	13		1
DoC	46	35	36	23	14	15	2		3		3	1		3	2	3	7	1		2		1	1	1				5	6	4	1	
DoD	1888	45	750	45	17	342	1	1	1	1	1	229	1	5	2	85	595	13							2	1		1	1		1	
DoE																																
DoI	152	16	16	74	10	17					5		2	1		19	35			13		5		1		5		7	1	7	1	
DoJ	152	128	114	102	43	47	9		6	3	1	11				34	20	2	1	1	1	2				5	3	24	7	9		
DoS	91	59	72	69	49	36	5		11		1	3	32	2	1	17	6	2	1	3		2	35	1			1	8	4	3		
EPA	35	29	32	17	7	19						4		2	2	2	7	1			2							3		24		
GSA	83	74	74	9	11	16	1		1		5	8		9	7	6	6	29		1										34		
HUD	75	25	25	54	41	44	1						5			34	11												1	26	1	
NARA	36	36	36	2	2	1			1					3	3	4	3	1									1		1	1		
NASA	57	57	57	57	24	40			1							44	1					1						2	7	2	2	
NRC	38	33	33	31	6	7	1				2	20	7	1	1	2	6	1				8						1		20		
RRB	21	1	2	12	3	16										1	6		3	7	1									3		
SSA	20	4	20	6	6	6	1		1			4				1	8	1		13							1		1	2		
SSS	3	3	3	3	2	2																										
Treasury	404	264	249	205	14	186	2				8	16	5	1	4	62	55	3	1	7	149	3	1			5		23	4	39	2	1
USDA	188		57	137	137	122	3									3	38	6	13	26		1						1	1	17	5	71
Grand Total	3400	833	1599	917	439	947	76	7	60	15	29	308	91	28	28	337	810	61	21	74	153	25	40	15	2	20	8	111	47	204	13	73

1. **DHS**: Due to the increased awareness and sensitivity of privacy and civil liberties concerns, the Coast Guard has implemented several identity management initiatives: 1) Handling and safeguarding personally identifiable information (PII); 2) agency-wide system use of an alternate identifier/Single Sign-on Login (SSL); and 3) protection of personal information within Information Sharing Environments (ISEs).

2. **DHS**:
   a. Follow the biometrics governance framework through supporting working groups.
   b. Follow recommendations within the Credentialing Framework Initiative, including:
      i. Design credentials to support multiple uses and environments.
      ii. Standardize vetting.
      iii. Establish electronic verification.
      iv. Make all immigration status checks electronic.
      v. Promote sharing and reuse of information, especially for enrollment data.
      vi. Establish processes for redress and updating that do not cause undue burden.
   c. Manage and merge, where appropriate credentialing programs such as First Responder credentials, HSPD 12, TWIC, US PASS, US VISIT, etc.

3. **DOC**: Compliance with the requirements of HSPD-12.

4. **DOC**: HSPD-12, 2-Factor Authentication, and E-Authentication E-Gov initiative PKI.

5. **DOD**: Develop and execute DOD Biometrics Strategy in concert with a DOD IdM Strategy Biometrics strategy based on the evolution of Biometric enterprise core capabilities for both friendly and other-than-friendly person.

6. **DOD**: With Release 2.1A (2 June 2008), 90-95 percent of the CAMS-ME Production user population will utilize PKE for access to the Production Portal application. Post 2.1A, the first or second quarter of FY2009, the remaining CAMS-ME Production users, will use PKE for access to the Production application. In addition, the Development and Quality environments will also use PKE.

7. **DOD**: Use of DOD CAC PKI for IT system access and transition to HSPD-12 complaint credentials.

8. **DOD**: Implementation of the HSPD-12 compliant Common Access Card (CAC), and Biometrics.

9. **DOD**: Initiatives are related to DOD programs.
10. **DOD**: CAC/FPIV integration — meeting the requirements of HSPD-12 to provide access to users based on CAC or FPIV credentials. JEDS — Integrating NCES' JEDS product to quickly identify users and privileges in real-time.
11. **DOD**: DOD SSN Reduction. DOD Privacy Impact Assessment/Privacy Act (PIA/PA).
12. **DOD**: JTF-GNO Accelerated PKI Implementation, HSPD-12 Personal Identity Verification, Smartcard/Biometrics/PKI Interoperability. Enterprise Identity Authentication Services, Global Enterprise Attribute Directory.
13. **DOD**: Our organization currently supports one application for personnel management purposes.
14. **DoE**: HSPD-12, E-Authentication.
15. **DOI**: Provisioning of PIV Cards as required by HSPD-12; Implementation of 2-factor authentication for remote access as required by OMB M-06-16.
16. **DOJ**: 1) Implementation of HSPD-12 PIV cards — Department-wide compliance w/ presidential mandate. 2) Department-wide enterprise directory and messaging consolidation — Consolidation of infrastructure required for cross-component interoperability for access control and electronic messaging. 3) Federated ID management — Piloting ID management brokering technologies to support heterogeneous access to data and systems to facilitate data sharing.
17. **DoS**: (1) HSPD-12 (Authentication); (2) IT Consolidation (Consolidation of Department Desktop services in the IRM Bureau); (3) SMART (automatically specifies classification and sensitivity on Department documents).
18. **EPA**: Enterprise IDM implementation includes: Streamlining and integrating agency directories, implementing HSPD-12 compliant smart cards for physical and logical access, improving user provisioning and deprovisioning and building capacity for identity federation.
19. **GSA**: HSPD-12 Agency Implementation (managed by HSPD-12 PMO). HSPD-12 PIV card services (managed by FAS HSPD-12 MSO). FICC (managed by OGP). eAuthentication implementation (managed by OCIO). Porta- based authentication, single sign-on (managed by PBS).
20. **HUD**: The Major identity management initiatives at the Dept, of HUD are compliance with HSPD-12 and FIPS 201 Personal Identity Verification.
21. **NARA**: Implementing HSPD-12, both for physical and logical access. Provide annual training for agency employees and others who come into contact with NARA owned PII while performing their official duties in accordance with OMB-M-07-16.
22. **NASA**: HSPD-12 and using the smartcard to enable multi-factor authentication to physical and logical assets; E-Gov E-Authentication.

23. **NRC**: IAM project currently underway includes requirements analysis, development of high-level IAM architecture, and strategic plan for agency to implement comprehensive IAM infrastructure.
24. **RRB**: Improving the agency's ability to meet identity management initiatives based upon legislative mandates.
25. **SSA**: The Social Security e-Authentication Steering Committee was formed to provide a focal point to oversee e-authentication policy, processes and technical solutions.
26. **SSS**: SSS is implementing RSA SecurID tokens in conjunction with normal login management.
27. **Treasury**: User ID and Password Login.
28. **Treasury**: SSN Reduction. 2 Factor Authentication. HSPD-12. E-Authentication.
29. **USDA**: HSPD-12, Enterprise Identity Management System, eAuthentication, Non-Employee Identity System (NEIS).

Data Call Results, Question 2b: What are the Agency's Top Three Identity Management Priorities?

1. **DHS**: 1) Handling and safeguarding PII; 2) agency-wide system use of an alternate identifier/SSL; and 3) protection of personal information within ISEs.
2. **DHS**: 1) Establish primary centers of excellence for all credentialing/screening/identity services; 2)Deploy HSPD 12 cards and associated PACS and LACS; and 3) Establish methods of working with state, local, and other populations for standardized law enforcement and disaster response identification.
3. **DOC**: Compliance with the requirements of HSPD-12.
4. **DOC**: 1) HSPD-12 physical and logical access; 2) Active Directory Implementation/Consolidation; and 3) Expand use of PKI.
5. **DOD**: 1) Counter-terrorism; 2) Interoperability; and 3) Friendly Persons IdM / HSPD-12.
6. **DOD**: No response.
7. **DOD**: 1) Protection of collected data while stored within Agency IT systems; 2) Protection of collected data when transmitted across Agency enclave boundaries; and 3) Detection when positive control of data is lost.
8. **DOD**: Develop an AF IdM Initial Capabilities Document (ICD), which will articulate a capability gap or set of capability gaps identified for a specific timeframe. The ICD will offer potential non-materiel and materiel solutions and support the analysis of alternatives and acquisition process for developing and delivering capability to the warfighter. The development of a PKI/CAC service-oriented architecture, and the deployment of biometrics and CAC capabilities for physical and logical access.
9. **DOD**: No answer.
10. **DOD**: Securing the PII of our existing user populace, ensuring that new users are properly vetted for the level of access they require, and researching new ways to ensure the integrity of our collected data.
11. **DOD**: SSN Reduction, and completion and submission of PIAs for systems containing personal identifiable information (PII).
12. **DOD**: 1) JTF-GNO Accelerated PKI Implementation; 2) HSPD-12 Personal Identity Verification Implementation; and 3) Global Enterprise Attribute Directory.
13. **DOD**: Accuracy, speed, ease of use.
14. **DOE**: Complete enterprise-wide HSPD-12 implementation
15. **DOI**: 1) HSPD-12 card deployment; 2) two-factor authentication for remote access; and 3) user provisioning systems/processes to integrate physical and logical access requirements.
16. **DOJ**: 1) Data security — Protection against loss and/or unauthorized access to departmental facilities, data and systems; 2) Protection of PII data

— Limit uses of PII data and ensure data is protected against loss, misuse and unauthorized use; and 3) Data sharing — Support interoperability and secure sharing of information assets for law enforcement, anti-terrorism and other business mission imperatives.

17. **DOS**: 1) Department's Public Key Infrastructure (PKI) and biometrics program; 2) IT Consolidation Program; and 3) Department's Employee Awareness Training Program and IT Security Professional Subject Matter Expert Training Program.

18. **EPA**: 1) Implement a centralized IDM solution for EPA; 2) ID normalization, reduction of redundancy of user ID; and 3) Establish EPA IDM requirements and Establish Policies framework.

19. **GSA**: 1) HSPD-12 PIV Card issuance to GSA staff; 2) Single signon agency wide; and 3) Maximum use of PIV cards for PACS/LACS.

20. **HUD**: 1) HSPD-12; 2) FIPS 201; and 3) the Personal Identity Verification process.

21. **NARA**: 1) Implementing the Federal Identity Card (FIC) by the 10/27/2008 deadline; 2) Implementing 2-Factor authentication by 9/30/2008; and 3) Evaluate and approve the GSA Privacy Impact Assessment for the USAccess Program powered by EDS Assured Identity.™

22. **NASA**: 1) Enabling 2 factor authentication to PII; 2) Encryption of PII in transit and at rest; and 3) Putting all PKI certs on smartcards.

23. **NRC**: 1) HSPD-12 2) logical access; and 3) Level 4 application authentication assurance.

24. **RRB**: 1) Improving identity management practices without impacting operational efficiencies; 2) Enhancing agency processes as it relates to identity management; and 3) Transforming business tasks by integrating improved identity management practices.

25. **SSA**: 1) Single Sign On; 2) Second Factor Authentication Protocol; and 3) Strengthening Identity Proofing.

26. **SSS**: 1) Network accounts; 2) Regularly changes passwords; and 3) RSA SecurID.

27. **Treasury**: 1) Desktop Security; 2) Login Security; and 3) Internet Security.

28. **Treasury**: 1) SSN Reduction; 2) HSPD-12; and 3) Registering, authenticating and managing identities of taxpayers effectively. Also, integration of Active Directory controls in all appropriate systems.

29. **USDA**: 1) HSPD-12; 2) Enterprise Identity Management System; and 3) Non-Employee Identity System.

1. **DHS:** There are myriad challenges to accomplish the agency's identity management goals requiring significant resources. The Coast Guard lacks resources to accomplish many of the requirements to ensure alignment with federal guidelines, e.g., reduction/elimination of SSNs, 2008 FISMA Reporting Requirements, National Intelligence Agency guidance regarding personal privacy concerns in ISEs, and the implementation of the 9/11 Commission Act of 2007 —Sections 803 and 804.

2. **DHS:** Interfacing with state and local entities for law enforcement and disaster response. Many disparate credentialing programs from agencies/organizations missions prior to the establishment of the Department. Often these missions overlap those of others within the Department that now have overlapping populations and distinct technologies.

3. **DOC:** Compliance with the requirements of HSPD-12.

4. **DOC:** Funding. Lack of common standards.

5. **DOD:** 1.Unfunded requirements. 2. Policy. 3. Integration and legacy systems.

6. **DOD:** Currently CAMS-ME users supply their SSN on their DD Form 2875. This causes concern re: identity theft. Future identity management initiatives should include the of other user-specific identification credentials to be used by security offices, rather than SSN.

7. **DOD:** Evolving nature of what specific data types apply, the rapid changes in the technology available to store, process, and transmit such data, and the security issues of trying to protect the data once gathered.

8. **DOD:** Keeping abreast of emerging and changing IdM technology, financial restraints, and educating IT owners and program managers. Instituting COIs and data labeling, privilege management, background vetting, and IdM and tokens for non-CAC eligible community. Authentication and authorization mechanisms as they deal with retirees, dependents, foreign nationals and coalition partners.

9. **DOD:** No answer.

10. **DOD:** The password rules surrounding non-CAC users for account maintenance requiring password and account updates every 60 days. Working with allied countries and their own internal security rules that conflict with DOD security requirements and procedures.

11. **DOD:** Interfaces with legacy systems. Identifying alternate unique identifiers that support security requirements for PII and alternate system architectures. Personnel training and compliance with privacy rules. Protecting PII in a system that is publicly accessible. User roles and permissions have been implemented.

12. **DOD:** Intra-/Inter-Agency HSPD-12 Logical and Physical Access Interoperability. Global Enterprise Attribute Directory Synchronization. Access Authorization, Privilege Management, Decisioning Services.

13. **DOD:** N/A.

14. **DOE:** Lack of federal standards; Integration of diverse legacy contractor environments to enable a centralized personnel environment.

15. **DOI:** Disparate systems supporting logical access, physical access, personnel and contractors; Lack of defined use cases for logical access; integration of identity management functions across organizational silos (e.g., HR, IT, Physical Security, Law Enforcement, First Responders, etc.); Multiple federal identity management initiatives (e.g., HSPD-12 and FRAC).

16. **DOJ:** 1) Enhancement and alignment of departmental infrastructure and services required to support department-wide usage of HSPD-12 PIV II smartcards for both physical and logical access in addition to advanced services such as digital signing and encryption. 2) State, local, tribal law enforcement access to DOJ systems and data.

17. **DOS:** Deployment and implementation of HSPD-12 world-wide specifically at overseas embassies and consulates is a continuing challenge. Vetting foreign nationals and other federal government agency staff. Funding concerns with ever increasing priority challenges.

18. **EPA:** Tying all existing user identity together including the PIV card to a single identity. Incorporate various level of security requirements by each system into a unified IDM solution. Selecting a COTS solution to integrate with EPA current environment. Funding of the entire IDM product.

19. **GSA:** Planning and coordination of agency investments. Lack of OMB direction on eAuthentication/HSPD-12 integration and interoperable cross agency HSPD-12 services. Lack of funding for identity management initiatives.

20. **HUD:** Obtaining adequate funding to acquire and thoroughly test new technologies.

21. **NARA:** 1. Funding/resources. 2. Complexity of the challenges for finding appropriate solutions.

22. **NASA:** 1) Integrating PKI encryption and signing certs onto the smartcard while retaining lifecycle management capabilities and key recovery capabilities; 2.) Identity vetting of partners in foreign countries; 3) Enterprise mechanisms to metatag data so that access can be limited based on aspects of a digital identity (e.g., protecting ITAR data from disclosure to unauthorized foreign nationals, understanding which credential was used by the individual to obtain access so assurance level can be determined); 4) Federations and trust, specifically maturity of identity federations and global mechanisms to enable use of identity federations, rules, common controls, compliance requirements and auditing for how to trust; 5) Securing services vs. just authenticating end users.

23. **NRC:** USAccess (GSA) card incompatibility with NRC Verisign PKI.

24. **RRB:** Integrating identity management processes with existing business systems.
25. **SSA:** Social Security is looking for safe and secure authentication solutions that meet NIST/OMB guidance that the public will use and successfully complete to access our Internet and automated phone transactions.
26. **SSS:** Funding shortages. Changing technical requirements, and unfunded mandates.
27. **Treasury:** Desktop Security, User turnover, Data Access.
28. **Treasury:** Single sign-on and uniform collection of identifiable information. Standing up an identity management group. Unfunded mandates. Need for single authoritative data source for employees/contractors, registering and authenticating taxpayers effectively.
29. **USDA:** Consolidation of user identities from distributed systems, validity of data in authoritative systems, lack of guaranteed unique identifiers.

Data Call Results, Question 2d: Has Your Organization Developed any "Use Cases" with Respect to Identity Management?

1. **DHS**: No. However, the Coast Guard has implemented the use of an Employee Identification (emplid) as an alternative to using SSNs in many applications.
2. **DHS**: No. None have been developed.
3. **DOC**: No.
4. **DOC**: Not at this time.
5. **DOD**: 35 use cases have been developed involving joint use of biometrics, and as many as 61 total are under development. Upon request, a link can be sent to the product postings.
6. **DOD**: No response.
7. **DOD**: SOPs drafted on when to report compromise/loss of data. SOPs and supporting policies can be provided.
8. **DOD**: See attached.
9. **DOD**: No response.
10. **DOD**: As a part of DTIC's participation in E-Authentication, a series of use-cases was developed with a focus on authentication within the E-Authentication Federation.
11. **DOD**: No.
12. **DOD**: 1) Army Volunteer PKI/IdM CONOPS; 2) Foreign National PKI/IdM CONOPS; 3) Biometrics PKI/IdM CONOPS; 4) RSA SecurID (OTP) CONOPS; 5) UID/PW Use CONOPS.
13. **DOD**: N/A.
14. **DOE**: No.
15. **DOI**: DOI has not yet developed any use cases for logical access. However, we expect to do this as part of the effort to enable two-factor authentication for remote access users. At that time, we will be happy to provide the use cases to the Task Force.

1. **DHS**: The Coast Guard participated in the SSN Tiger Team and the Homeland Security Information Network (HSIN). The SSN Tiger Team is a federal government collaborative effort to determine a solution for eliminating the use of SSNs and the legislative requirements to appeal EO 9397 (law signed by President Roosevelt in 1946 enacting the use of SSNs). Additionally, the Coast Guard was integral in establishing the privacy framework for HSIN, an ISE established after 9/11 to combat terrorism nationwide.

2. **DHS**: Smart Card Alliance, NSTC Subcommittee on Biometrics, International Conference on Biometrics and Ethics, Biometrics Security Consortium (BSC), Biometrics Coordination Group, US Army biometrics Task Force, Interagency Advisory Board (credentialing), Defense Science Board Task Force on Defense Biometrics, Federal Interoperability and Credentialing Committee (FICC).

3. **DOC**: BEA participates in the Department's HSPD-12 implementation group.

4. **DOC**: Federal Identity Credential Committee, E-Authentication E-Gov initiative, and HSPD-12.

5. **DOD**: Defense Enrollment Eligibility Reporting System.

6. **DOD**: NSTC Subcommittee on Biometrics and Identity Management, ISO/IEC/JTC1/SC27 (IT Security Techniques), ISO/IEC SC 37 (Biometrics), OASIS, NCITS M1 (Biometrics).

7. **DOD**: No response.

8. **DOD**: N/A.

9. **DOD**: AF IdM office is working with several AF functional communities to deploy biometrics and CAC capabilities for physical and logical access. The AF is also engaged with the DOD Biometrics Task Force, the DOD PKI office, the Defense Manpower Data Center, The Air Force Personnel Center, OSD/NII and the National Security Agency.

10. **DOD**: No response.

11. **DOD**: DTIC participates in the Federal E-Authentication program. Working with GSA, DTIC has the capacity to accept identified and approved credentials from commercial vendors for access to resources identified as being available to E-Authentication participants.

12. **DOD**: None.

13. **DOD**: DOD Identity Protection and Management Senior Coordinating Group (IPMSCG), DOD PKI Certificate Policy Management Working Group (CPMWG), Evaluation Program Technical Working Group

(EPTWG), Attribute Based Access Control Working Group (ABACWG), and Federal PKI Policy Authority (FPKI PA).

14. **DOD**: ID Management and Protection, DMDC Working groups, AFCEA, CTST.

15. **DOE**: HSPD-12, E-Authentication.

16. **DOI**: Federal Identity Credentialing Committee (FICC); GSA PKI Working Group; GSA E-Authentication Steering Committee; GSA E-Authentication Technical Working Group

17. **DOJ**: 1) Federated ID management pilot with the Directorate of National Intelligence; 2) Participation in the GSA HSPD-12 architecture working group (AWG); 3) Participation in the Federal Identity Credentialing Committee (FICC); and 4) Participation in the Interagency Advisory Board (IAB).

18. **DOS**: CNSS, Federal PKI Working Group, FICC, and FPKI.

19. **EPA**: EPA is not participating in interagency or industry efforts at this time.

20. **GSA**: FICC (Federal Identity Credentialing Committee), SmartCard IAB (Industry Advisory Board), ISC (Interagency Security Committee), SmartCard Alliance (SCA), and Security Industry Alliance (SIA).

21. **HUD**: The Dept. of HUD participates on the Federal Identity Credentialing Committee.

22. **NARA**: As described in 2d, NARA has the IAA with the GSA MSO and their primary contractor EDS for identity management. We have no agency-specific initiatives in this area from our personnel security perspective; we use OPM to conduct our background investigations which helps support the identity management agreement with GSA.

23. **NASA**: 1) Federal PKI Policy Authority: Karen Petraska, Susan Levine; 2) Federal Identity Credentialing Committee: Karen Petraska, Will Morrison; 3) Government Smartcard Interagency Advisory Board: Tim Baldridge.

24. **NRC**: Attend workshops and seminars including FICC.

25. **RRB**: At this time, the agency does not have the resources to participate in interagency and industry collaborative efforts.

26. **SSA**: Social Security was an early partner in the GSA e-Authentication Federation. As part of this federation, Social Security partners with GSA and Fidelity Investments to allow users to change their address a once successfully e-authenticated by Fidelity. GSA is the gateway between SSA and Fidelity.

27. **SSS**: FISMA initiative and FISMA auditing.

28. **Treasury**: None.

29. **Treasury**: HSPD-12, Treasury Privacy Committee, and Cyber Security Sub Council.

30. **USDA**: HSPD-12, authentication.

Data Call Results, Question 2f: What are the Biggest Challenges you Face in Addressing Privacy Concerns Related to Identity Management Systems?

1. **DHS**: The Coast Guard's biggest challenge addressing privacy concerns related to identity management systems is lack of resources needed for human capital, fiscal funding, etc., to allow the development of Integrated Project Teams for execution of segmented studies to address sensitive information in a number of areas.
2. **DHS**: Sharing investments and information across programs without creating a "Master DHS Database."
3. **DOC**: Secure storage of personal information collected as a result of the implementation of the requirements of HSPD-12.
4. **DOC**: Funding. Divergent technical standards.
5. **DOD**: 1) Separate myth from reality; required, legal, perception; 2) Expanding information sharing in the information sharing environment while simultaneously safeguarding personally identifiable information; and 3) Rapid technology proliferation is outpacing policy implementation.
6. **DOD**: No response.
7. **DOD**: There is no established audit trail for tracking data from its first collection through its subsequent use during the course of its "ownership" by the government.
8. **DOD**: Financial restraints, educating IT owners and program managers, and keeping abreast of emerging and changing IdM technology.
9. **DOD**: 1) Compliance with privacy laws; 2) Staff awareness and training.
10. **DOD**: Balancing the requirement to log and monitor usage to ensure that the user is using the site properly without infringing on privacy.
11. **DOD**: 1) Interfaces with legacy systems; 2) Identifying alternate unique identifiers that support security requirements for PII and alternate system architectures; 3) Personnel training and compliance with privacy rules; 4) Protecting PII in a system that is publicly accessible. User roles and permissions have been implemented.
12. **DOD**: 1) Physical and/or Logical Separation of Public and Private Data; 2) Consistent Application of Policy Guidelines throughout the Enterprise; 3) Process Synchronization and Sustainment throughout the Enterprise.
13. **DOD**: A unique identifier on all media of current CAC/PIV and other agency IDs to index dbs with.
14. **DOE**: Cyber security, system integration (development and policy/business rule integration).
15. **DOI**: DOI will manage privacy concerns for identity management systems using the existing processes and requirements for developing PIAs and SORNs.

16. **DOJ**: General reluctance on the part of DOJ bureaus to have any PII stored outside of the agency. Applies to use in other agency operated lines of business applications and managed services, such as the GSA HSPD-12 managed service. This is not preventing use of such systems, however the department addresses these concerns time and again with our components.

17. **DOS**: DOS already collected required privacy data in order to obtain DoS identity credentials, the only new challenge associated with HSPD-12 was the capturing, storing, and forwarding of biometric data (fingerprints).

18. **EPA**: Achieving single sign-on across the enterprise.

19. **GSA**: 1) Training for staff handling PII; 2) Protection of stored PII data.

20. **HUD**: The biggest challenges the Dept. of HUD faces is the ability to provide a secure communications and application environment.

21. **NARA**: NARA's identity management system is in the developmental phase. At this time we are evaluating the privacy implications involved in the development and maintenance of our information management system.

22. **NASA**: 1) Community misconceptions about what is on the smartcards, and; 2) Implementing and enforcing role based access mechanisms.

23. **NRC**: Assignment of data responsibility.

24. **RRB**: Maintaining consistent privacy policies with multiple content repository environments and data sources.

25. **SSA**: Social Security has a goal to offer more electronic services while balancing risks associated with the improper disclosure of personal information. The difficulty lies in determining how much risk the agency is willing to take to make our electronic services attractive to the general public in a manner that adequately protects personal privacy.

26. **SSS**: Funding shortages. Changing technical requirements, and unfunded mandates.

27. **Treasury**: User turnover.

28. **Treasury**: Cost, Complexity, Funding, Competing Priorities. While security and privacy usually work well together, with often overlapping goals, Identity Management is one area where security needs and the rights to privacy can come into conflict.

29. **USDA**: Lack of globally unique identifiers and identity integration in legacy applications

Data Call Results, Question 2g: Have you Developed any Policies or Procedures Related to Addressing Privacy Concerns Raised by Identity Management Systems?

1. **DHS**: Yes. The Coast Guard has developed policies and procedures to address privacy concerns raised by identity management systems, e.g., FOI/Privacy Acts Manual, Safeguarding PII, Privacy Incident Response, Notification, and Reporting Procedures for PII; privacy concerns are also addressed in any Coast Guard directive relating to Health, Financial, and Information Security.
2. **DHS**: Each system is required to undergo a Privacy Threat Assessment, which determines whether a PIA, SORN, or other measures are required. Systems with identity data are secured using standards based on FISMA.
3. **DOC**: Yes.
4. **DOC**: Departmental privacy policy and policy on 2-Factor authentication.
5. **DOD**: 1) Privacy Act compliance and complementing support of internal structure and guidance; 2) System of Record Notice; and 3) Updated draft Privacy Impact Assessment.
6. **DOD**: No response.
7. **DOD**: No.
8. **DOD**: We are unaware of any privacy concerns raised by identity management systems or tools. The Air Force has policy and procedures to protect PII at rest and in transient. We also have policy (Air Force Instruction (AFI) 33-332, Privacy Act Program), which requires system owners and developers assess privacy through the early stages of system development.
9. **DOD**: Modeled on DOD and other Federal Agency Best Practices.
10. **DOD**: We adhere to the security policies and requirements as directed by the DOD.
11. **DOD**: No. However, OUSD(AT&L) ARA is developing an SSN Reduction and Management Plan.
12. **DOD**: Army Regulation (AR) 25-1, Army Regulation (AR) 25-2, DODD 8500.1, DODI 8500.2, DODI 8520.2.
13. **DOD**: No.
14. **DOE**: No.
15. **DOI**: DOI has not developed specific policies beyond those that cover privacy requirements for any system. System of Records Notices (SORNs) and Privacy Impact Assessments (PIAs) have been published as required for all identity management systems.
16. **DOJ**: Yes. DOJ has developed Privacy Impact Assessment guidance and templates.
17. **DOS**: Diplomatic Security reports Privacy Impact Assessments (PIA) were written and submitted to OMB in support of HSPD-12.

18. **EPA**: No specific privacy concerns have been identified at this time.
19. **GSA**: Yes, GSA Privacy Act Program in Office of the Chief Human Capital Officer (OCHO). See SORNS for all GSA IT systems holding PII data. Incorporated policies into HSPD-12 business process.
20. **HUD**: HUD has developed policies and procedures related to addressing privacy concerns raised by identity management systems.
21. **NARA**: NARA has issued policies and procedures necessary to effect a sound privacy program. Those policies will also apply to the identity management system. NARA will develop additional policy guidance and implementation plans as we learn more about the functionality of the system.
22. **NASA**: As required by federal directives.
23. **NRC**: No.
24. **RRB**: The agency has not yet completed development of any policies or procedures related to addressing privacy concerns raised by identity management systems; however, we would be interested in receiving available information on the topic.
25. **SSA**: Yes. Social Security recently updated its regulations to address a number of privacy concerns, including those raised by identity management solutions. We issued a specific regulation on verifying identity electronically and an additional provision on electronic disclosures. We also published a provision on privacy impact assessments. In addition, the Social Security Information Systems Security Handbook contains additional guidance and policies relating to identity management.
26. **SSS**: Yes — HQ orders and directives to incorporate FIPS, FISMA, and SP800 series recommendations.
27. **Treasury**: No.
28. **Treasury**: Some bureaus have updated their policies.
29. **USDA**: Yes. Effort is focused on minimization of the use and storage of PII data first, then providing appropriate security around PII that must be used and maintained.

*Data Call Results, Question 3a: Is your Agency Funding any Science and Technology Re-
search Efforts in the Area of Identity Management?*

1. **DOJ**: CJIS Biometrics Center of Excellence (FBI), CJIS Next Gen Identification (FBI).
2. **DOD**: PSA / DDB.
3. **DOD**: Pursuing funding to pilot a BIdM project at Wright-Patterson AFB,
   OH.

1. **DHS**: Recommend the Task Force explore the use of an alternate identifier vice use of the SSN and promulgate policy in alignment with the Office of Management and Budget (OMB) guidance to reduce/eliminate the use of SSN. The rationale is if the NSTC Task Force mission is to resolve/eliminate the numerous identity management technologies, standards and related plans that are being developed independently at the application and sector-specific levels (such as telecommunications, border security, financial services, identity theft, etc.), then the establishment of an alternate identifier will positively contribute to the technological needs government-wide. Clearly, the Coast Guard would benefit from a coordinated federal effort, as this would allow the agency to totally transition its systems from using SSNs to the use of an alternate identifier, fostering compliance with OMB guidelines, ensuring privacy protection, and enabling individuals to exercise their identities securely. Implementing this approach would undoubtedly reduce the overall cost to the federal government.

2. **DOD**: Task Force review Defense Manpower Data Center (DMDC) SSN/PII Datacall and Analysis Report.

3. **DOD**: The need to come to terms with a standard lexicon of what constitutes Identity Management data and its relationship with Personally Identifiable Information if different.

4. **DOD**: No.

5. **DOD**: Some of the other U.S. departments (e.g., Education, Housing and Urban Development, Interior, and Labor) should be included, as they probably have systems containing federal information in identifiable form.

6. **DOI**: DOI fully supports the need to develop use cases for Logical Access Controls (LACS).

7. **EPA**: Any materials produced by the Task Force should reflect the following operating principles: 1) Access to PII should be role-based and limited to the minimum amount needed to perform whatever the necessary function; and 2) Any PII that is transmitted from one point to another should have proper safeguards in place to protect the information.

8. **GSA**: Please improve description of breakdown for Question 1e. You should provide a clearer explanation of what each category includes, and also add an "Other" column just for checking total match column 1a.

9. **SSA**: To meet the challenges of delivering high quality services to citizens, the SSA is aggressively pursuing a range of electronic service delivery methods as part of our strategic planning. These methods require strong identity management capabilities to ensure the public confidence.

SSA recommends that the NSTC Task Force consider IdM activity from a broad perspective that includes citizen oriented services as well as counter terrorism. The Task Force should proceed as expeditiously as possible in order to provide agencies with standards, guidance, etc. that may be integrated into agencies' planning and architectures.

10. **Treasury**: Standardize identity management requirements and fund identity management initiatives.

11. **USDA**: Designate OPM as the authoritative source of Person Identifiers across the entire federal government.

12. **DOD**: Identity Management is a process that overarches numerous organizations and equities involved in technology and end-user processes. There is a need for an enduring governance structure to routinely facilitate cross-organizational collaboration in this area, both at the federal government — wide/interagency level, and in major federal organizations with complex IdM-related missions, such as the Department of Defense. Important to coordinate efforts across the federal government for best results and cost effectiveness.

Annex H Additional Information from PIA Assessment

This annex provides the results of the PIA assessment conducted by the Task Force. A PIA is an E-Government Act-mandated analysis of how PII is handled by electronic systems of the federal government. A PIA has three goals:

1. To ensure handling of PII conforms to privacy protection requirements.
2. To determine the risks and effects of collecting, maintaining and disseminating PII through an electronic system.
3. To evaluate protections and alternatives for handling PII to limit potential privacy risks.

The PIA process allows systems designers and programs sponsors to approach privacy systemically, in the design stage, by thinking through, and laying out, the ways in which sensitive information is to be collected, used and stored within government systems. This process adds to the desired tone in government's management of privacy by allowing for transparency in this analysis, through the generation and publication of PIAs for each such program.

The Task Force's effort to collect and analyze all publicly available federal government-created PIAs had several aims. The first of these was to systematically investigate the types of data collected by electronic systems across the government. Additionally, the Task Force sought to identify similarities and differences across PIAs toward better understanding the policies and privacy protections implemented by the various U.S. agencies generating PIAs. Ultimately, this collection and analysis effort hopes to use PIAs to identify and understand existing efforts in IdM across the federal government.

For this effort, PIAs were used as the points of analysis for several reasons. First, because their creation and dissemination is mandated by the E-Government Act of 2002, a majority of created PIAs are readily available from government Web sites. Additionally, because PIAs follow a standardized format for dissemination, they are easily comparable to each other. For the purposes of this analysis, only publicly available PIAs were collected and analyzed; PIAs for sensitive or classified systems were not requested nor included.

The Task Force collected 1,595 PIAs, largely from agency Web sites, in order to determine what IdM-related information could be obtained. In order to help constrain the collection effort, we focused on obtaining PIAs from only the agencies represented on the Task Force. The list of agency PIAs initially collected from agency Web sites was provided to the representatives of each agency on the Task Force, in order to confirm that our collection of PIAs was accurate and complete. Confirmation was received from the majority of agencies queried.

These PIAs were then converted to PDF format (when required) and compiled them into a searchable catalog using Adobe Acrobat. For each PIA, we also captured the bureau (e.g., U.S. Mint and IRS for the Treasury Department) and documented this information in an Excel spreadsheet for easy reference.

However, it must be noted that though our collection of PIA documents was nearly comprehensive and, thus, the following keyword analyses of the collected PIAs should be considered complete, there does exist additional PIA documents that were excluded from the IdM Task Force review due to their being sensitive (e.g., For Official Use Only) or classified. As a result, overall conclusions about the use of these terms in the PIA documents collected cannot be considered without the caveat that for many of these terms there may exist additional U.S. Government programs, departments, or systems that do likely collect data on or use the terms below, thereby rendering any conclusion we might draw from this PIA analysis about the usage of these terms and the data collections they entail across the federal government somewhat incomplete.

The Task Force identified thirteen terms to be used for analysis of the PIA database: biometric(s), DNA, fingerprint(s), facial, identity, iris, personal identification number (PIN), discretionary access control, mandatory access control, role-based access control, token, two-factor authentication, and voice.

The list of terms is skewed toward those that are related to biometrics, in part because the field of biometrics is a rich source of terminology that is identity-specific.

Table H-1 summarizes the results of the keyword analysis. Of the 13 terms that were analyzed across 1,595 PIA documents, Table H-1 also lists the total number of instances (i.e., "hits") of the term across all PIA documents, the total number of PIA documents that include the term at least once, the number of false positive instances (e.g., a search on the term "iris" resulted in one of the 72 hits being a reference to a database management system with an acronym of "IRIS"), and some summary observations.

Term	Instances	# of Documents	False Positives	Summary Observations
Biometric(s)	1174	131	32	99 PIAs use the term biometric; Half relate to Personal Identity Verification (PIV) card; Half are DHS and DOJ systems.
DNA	82	27	15	12 PIAs use the term DNA; Many are DoS systems.
Fingerprint(s)	437	81	12	69 PIAs use the term fingerprints; Most associated with PIV cards.
Facial	54	12	0	12 PIAs use the term facial; Four use the term in relation to facial images collected for PIV cards; Eight refer to the collection of facial images for identification, security, or immigration systems.
Identity	1087	218	18	200 PIAs use the term identity; Most relate to allowing a user access to a particular system or database.
Iris	72	15	7	8 PIAs discuss the use of iris scans; Most are TSA programs.
Personal Identification Number (PIN)	58	43	0	43 PIAs use the term PIN; Mostly used for access control.
Discretionary Access Control (DAC)	15	9	2	7 uses of the term DAC; All are general in nature, not specific.
Mandatory Access Control (MAC)	11	5	0	5 uses of the term MAC; Most are DHS systems.
Role-based Access Control (RBAC)	122	59	0	59 PIAs use the term RBAC; Most describe database protection controls.
Token	23	15	0	15 PIAs use the term token; Half refer to RSA SecurID tokens.
Two-factor Authentication	23	10	0	10 PIAs discuss two-factor authentication; Most associated with PIV cards.
Voice	59	24	18	6 PIAs use the term voice for authentication; Most use the term "voice print" for biometric purposes

Table H-1. Summary of Keyword Results

The principal observation of this analysis was that few PIAs include the use of terms that relate to biometrics (e.g., iris, voice, facial, DNA). We conclude that few of the programs that are required to produce PIAs are using biometric technology. The Task Force notes that while the PIA analysis is very helpful for its intended purpose, augmenting the PIAs with specific identity-related questions would provide much more insight into the current state of practice in how identity is managed and implemented within the Executive Branch.

A Privacy Impact Assessment (PIA) is, according to the Office of Management and Budget's Guidance for Implementing the Privacy Procedures of the E-Government Act of 2002:

> …An analysis of how (personally identifiable) information is handled: (i) to ensure handling conforms to applicable legal, regulatory, and policy requirements regarding privacy, (ii) to determine the risks and effects of collecting, maintaining and disseminating information in identifiable form in an electronic information system, and (iii) to examine and evaluate protections and alternative processes for handling information to mitigate potential privacy risks.[36]

The E-Government Act of 2002[37] requires that any federal government agency wishing to develop an electronic system to "collect, maintain, or disseminate" personally identifiable information (PII)[38] about an individual must conduct a PIA. In sum, the government requires the creation of PIAs when a

---

[36] M-03-22. OMB Guidance for Implementing the Privacy Provisions of the E-Government Act of 2002. Web site, available from: http://www.whitehouse.gov/omb/memoranda/m03-22 html#2

[37] A summary of the E-Government Act of 2002 can be found at this Web site: http://www.whitehouse.gov/omb/egov/g-4-act.html, as can a link to the full-text of the Act.

[38] Personally identifiable information is defined by OMB M-03-22 as "information in an IT system or online collection: (i) that directly identifies an individual (e.g. name, address, social security number or other identifying number or code, telephone number, email address, etc.) or (ii) by which an agency intends to identify specific individuals in conjunction with other data elements, i.e., indirect identification. (These data elements may include a combination of gender, race, birth date, geographic indicator, and other descriptors)."

The 2002 E-Gov Act as "any representation of information that permits the identity of an individual to whom the information applies to be reasonably inferred by either direct or indirect means." Information "permitting the physical or online contacting of a specific individual" (see section 208(b)(1)(A)(ii)(II)) is the same as "information in identifiable form."

system will use PII and through the PIA, the government aims to mitigate any privacy risk before the system is deployed.

KEYWORD ANALYSIS

Iris

A search for "iris" returned 15 PIA documents containing the term "iris." Of those 15 documents, seven were false positives (e.g., references to database systems such as IRIS and IRISV3), revenue control systems (i.e., the Alcohol and Tobacco Tax and Trade Bureau's Integrated Revenue Information System) or HHS time management systems). The remaining eight documents referencing the term "iris" do so in regard to the collection of biometric data from a scan of a human iris.

Of the eight PIAs making at least one reference to biometric-related "iris," all but one are for Transportation Security Administration (TSA) programs; the last is for Federal Bureau of Investigation (FBI)/DHS data sharing module that has the potential to collect biometric data, including iris scans.

Iris is discussed as one element of biometric data, usually alongside fingerprint data. Iris scans are considered voluntary biometric data for the TSA PIAs – secondary biometric data used for evaluative purposes, (or in the case of the Registered Traveler Pilot, for research purposes to develop a biometric iris standard with National Institute of Standards and Technology (NIST)).

From this analysis we conclude that few publicly visible programs within the U.S. government collect or seek to collect iris scans as biometric data in any capacity, and those that do currently intend to use it in a secondary capacity only. With that in mind, we also note that our PIA analysis indicates that iris scans are currently limited to the TSA, and mostly to the Registered Traveler Program in an entirely voluntary and non-limiting capacity.

Fingerprint

A search for "fingerprint," which also returned results for "fingerprints," revealed 81 PIA documents mentioning the term "fingerprint" or "fingerprints." A closer analysis unearthed twelve incorrect match results — all from the Department of Justice/FBI — which occur due to the way the PIAs were captured (in capturing PIA documents from HTML, we inadvertently and unavoidably also captured extraneous text, which in this case included a link to "fingerprint" not relevant to the PIAs).

After discounting the incorrect matches, a total of 69 PIAs referencing the term fingerprint were collected for 10 departments. We roughly categorized the PIAs into 3 categories:

- PIAs referencing fingerprint collection activities to be used exclusively for internal Human Resources (HR) or Personal Identity Verification (PIV) card systems

- PIAs for systems that require the collection of fingerprints as a form of biometric data

- PIAs for systems that contain and pass along fingerprint and other biometric data but do not seek to collect it

For 5 of the 10 departments with PIAs referencing "fingerprint," the PIAs could be categorized into PIAs using fingerprints for HR or PIV card systems (15 PIAs in 5 departments). For the other five departments, the majority of PIAs referencing fingerprints in a biometric data collection capacity were found in DHS (34 of 40 PIAs are for DHS programs). PIAs for systems containing and transmitting fingerprint data were more evenly distributed across DHS, DOD, DOJ/FBI, and DOS.

A search for "fingerprints" found 67 documents with 439 instances of the term used. 52 of those 67 documents also contain the term "fingerprint," the other 15 represent PIAs that were not captured in the above search for "fingerprint." Cross-referencing PIAs that describe the collection or transmission of "fingerprint" or "fingerprints" indicate that, after disallowing for false positives, 83 PIAs captured by our collection efforts use the term "fingerprint" or "fingerprints." Of these 83 PIAs, all but one refer to fingerprints in the most well-known sense of the word; that is, the imprint of fingertips captured on paper or digital image. The outlying PIA — for the Centers for Disease Control and Prevention (CDC) PulseNet program — discusses the collection of "DNA fingerprints" — unique DNA profiles used in a manner similar to typical fingerprints. Overall, we found that a limited number of PIA documents across the federal government mention the terms "fingerprint" or "fingerprints." Those that do mention either term do so primarily in reference to the capture and dissemination of biometric data, with the remainder mentioning the terms in relation to the use of fingerprint data in meeting Homeland Security Presidential Direction 12 (HSPD-12) requirements for PIV cards.

Two Factor Authentication

A search for "two factor authentication," which also returned the variant "two-factor authentication," returned 10 PIA documents referencing the term. The 10 PIAs mentioning two-factor authentication originate in multiple departments, including DOC (National Oceanic and Atmospheric Administration (NOAA)), DHS, DOD (Air Force), DOJ, GSA, HHS (National Institute of Health (NIH)), National Science Foundation (NSF), and Department of the Treasury.

Several of the PIAs using the term two-factor authentication do not offer an explicit definition for the term, or specify which "factors" are required for authentication. About half of the PIA documents discuss two-factor authentication as part of a strategy to limit access to personal information stored in government computer systems; the remaining half describe two-factor identification in the context of PIV/Common Access Card (CAC)/Transportation Worker Identification Credential (TWIC) cards and the PII collected to support the security of those cards.

Five of the 10 PIAs discussing two-factor authentication mention a HSPD-12-based identity card as one of the two factors required for authentication. Other factors mentioned by the PIAs include biometric data, a PIN, an RSA token, and a password.

Biometric (includes biometrics)

A search for "biometric," which also returned results for "biometrics," returned 131 PIA documents mentioning the term(s) "biometric(s)." Over half of the PIAs collected mentioning the terms biometric or biometrics (or both) are for DHS databases or systems. The remainder is from DOJ, GSA, HHS, NASA, DOS, and the VA. Most (20) of the VA PIAs (22 total) mentioning biometrics should be recorded as false positives, since they include the text biometric but it is not referenced to the actual content of the PIA; similarly, twelve of the 15 DOJ PIAs discussing biometrics do so without any reference to the actual content of the PIA and should be considered False Positives.

To generalize briefly, PIAs from departments other than DHS and DOJ use the term biometric generally in reference to data collected for compliance with HSPD-12 rather than for security/immigration/criminal investigation purposes, whereas DHS and DOJ PIAs referencing biometrics do so for non-PIV card purposes.

Drilling further into the use of the terms "biometric" and "biometrics" in DHS PIAs, we find that in some PIAs the term biometric is well-defined, referencing the various types of biometric data collected (e.g., fingerprints, voice prints, iris scans), while in others these data are not described. The DHS PIAs collected describe several different uses of biometric data between and within DHS databases and systems. For example, in some DHS PIAs, biometric data is used as an access control data point; that is, iris scans are used for physical access controls and are stored in a database.

Identity

A search for "identity" returned 218 PIA documents mentioning the term "identity." Those PIAs referencing the term "identity" were created by multiple departments, including: DOC, DHS, DOJ, FTC, GSA, HHS, NASA, NSF, SSA, State, DOT, Treasury, and the VA. The VA again features multiple PIAs that register a false positive for the actual use of the term "identity" — as for the term "biometric" above, these PIAs registering false positives include the term we searched for as part of a generic section header, but did not actually report use of the term for the actual system for which the PIA was created for — leaving approximately 200 PIAs with valid references to the term identity.

Generally, PIAs described three types of systems/databases from which the use of the term identity within the PIAs collected stems: to verify identities, to authenticate identities, and to communicate an identity or elements of an identity. On the broadest level, the majority of PIAs focus on the authentication of identities in relation to allowing a user access to a particular system or database. Generally, only DHS, State, and DOJ/FBI PIAs discuss the verification of identity in a criminal/national security sense, or discuss the transmission of identity elements across systems.

Facial

A search for "facial" returned 12 PIA documents mentioning the term. Of the 12 PIAs collected, four departments are represented (DHS, DOJ, HHS, and the VA). Four of the 12 PIAs reference the term in relation to facial images collected for PIV cards systems in accordance with HSPD-12; the other eight PIAs refer to the collection of facial images for identification, security, or immigration systems.

Interestingly, facial images are not referred to as biometric data by any of the PIAs, but rather as biographical data by several. For several of the DHS databases collecting facial images for security/identification purposes, facial images are treated as PII and are governed by specific privacy protections.

Personal Identification Number (includes PIN)

A search for the term "personal identification number," which overlapped with a search for the term "PIN," returned 43 PIA documents mentioning one or both of the terms. The 43 PIAs collected for systems discussing the term personal identification number come from several federal government departments including DOC, DHS, DOD, DOJ, GSA, SSA, and Department of the Treasury (mostly the Internal Revenue Service (IRS)).

The SSA uses PINs as a form of access control to administration databases containing PII of either employees or citizens, requiring that employees accessing SSA databases to possess and apply a PIN for access.

For PIAs for systems and databases of the IRS, PINs are not used as a form of access control, but treated usually as a unique identifier, or an element of an electronic identity, and are thus included in PIAs because they are considered to be PII.

For PIAs from non-SSA and non-IRS systems, PINs are used for authentication purposes, usually as part of a PIV card, and are considered more as biographical data and less as biometric data. Overall, we found that a limited number of PIA documents across the federal government mention the use of personal identification numbers (PINs). The majority of PIAs referencing PINs do so as a form of access control rather than as a form of biographical data, and given the number of PIA documents collected mentioning some type of access control system, we anticipate that personal identification numbers will continue to be implemented in this capacity into the future.

Token

A search for "token" returned 15 PIA documents mentioning the term "token." The 15 PIAs collected that mention the term Token are from systems in five departments: DHS, DOJ, HHS, Department of the Treasury, and the VA. The PIAs reference two "types" of tokens; in one sense, tokens refer to a small physical media item embedded with a chip that provides a set piece of information necessary to authenticate the access of the item's carrier to a system; in the other sense, tokens refer to a unique piece of identifying information — but not a physical item — that allows a user access to a secured system. Several of the DHS PIAs refer to this latter use of tokens in describing a form of access control as including "two token authentication."

Of the PIAs that refer to tokens as a physical item displaying a unique identifier, about half reference the popular RSA SecurID tokens; the remainder only refer to "access control" tokens or simply "secure tokens."

Voice

A search for the term "voice" returned 24 PIA documents mentioning the term in some capacity. However, we were only interested in the use of the term "voice" in an authentication or verification capacity — we were not interested in PIAs for voicemail and automated voice systems. We found that the majority of the 24 PIAs collected that reference the term voice do so in reference to automated telephone systems used to provide information to users or to voice-mail systems — only six of the 24 PIAs collected referenced the term voice with regard to authentication or verification purposes. We collected PIAs which included the term voice from seven federal government departments, including: DOC, DHS, DOJ, HHS, DOS, Department of the Treasury (IRS only), and the VA. However, only DHS, DOJ, and DOS featured PIAs regarding systems in security/crime/defense-sectors; it is those PIAs that referenced the term voice with regard to identity/privacy-related issues.

For those six PIAs referencing the term voice as used for authentication purposes, two were from DHS, two from DOJ (both FBI), and two from DOS. Each of these PIAs treats voices — most use the term voice print — as a piece of biometric data, equal to a fingerprint.

Role(-)Based Access Control

A search for "role based access control, which also included a search for "role-based access control," returned 59 PIA documents referencing the term "role(-)based access control." All of those 59 PIAs discuss the use of role-based (role based) access controls to limit or otherwise manage access to Department databases. The majority of the PIAs mentioning role based access control, 35, are for DHS systems. Most, if not all, of the DHS PIAs discussing role-based access controls do so in relation to protected databases containing PII for security rather than internal/administrative/human-resources purposes.

Additionally, unlike the other departments referring to role based access controls in their available PIAs (DOJ [12], HHS [3], DOS [1], Department of the Treasury/IRS [8]), DHS does not define the roles relevant to the access controls, likely due to the difference in types of databases utilizing/requiring role-based access controls. That is, the PIAs for DOJ, HHS, DOS, and Department of the Treasury/IRS generally refer to role-based access controls for internal/administrative/HR-specific databases as opposed to the databases referenced by DHS PIAs.

Discretionary Access Control

A search for "discretionary access control" returned nine PIA documents referencing the term. These nine PIA documents collected mention the use of discretionary access controls in the context of limiting or otherwise managing access to U.S government databases. These nine PIAs come from several departments, including Department of the Treasury (IRS and non-IRS), DOJ, DOD, and the VA. The two PIAs from DOS mentioning discretionary access control do so only in their list of acronyms, and should be considered "false positives" for useful information.

Most of the non-FP PIAs mentioning discretionary access control do so without any explanation of how said controls would be applied and to which aspect of the system analyzed for the PIA. Several of the PIAs (three) noted only that discretionary access controls were built into the operating systems of their computer systems — Windows 2003 and Windows NT. Those PIAs that did discuss the application of discretionary access controls did so in reference to a type of access control that allows users of a system to access only selected bits of information based on pre-set user information.

Mandatory Access Control

A search for the term "mandatory access control" returned five PIA documents. Four of the five PIA documents mentioning Mandatory Access Controls are for DHS systems; the fifth comes out of the IRS. While the IRS PIA does not explain how said access controls are applied or what their purpose is (beyond controlling access, of course), the DHS PIAs go into more detail.

According to the DHS PIA documents mentioning the term, mandatory access controls, as opposed to discretionary access controls, provide users access to systems on a "demonstrated need-to-know" basis, and is enforced on multiple levels. Additionally, the DHS PIAs specify that mandatory access controls specify that multiple approvals are needed for users to gain or modify their access to systems with such controls — a stronger level of access control than discretionary or role-based controls. Overall, however, like discretionary access controls, mandatory access controls were not mentioned by even a small minority of PIA documents.

DNA

A search for "DNA" revealed 27 PIA documents mentioning the term. A closer analysis unearthed 15 false positives — all from the DOJ/FBI, due to the way the PIAs were captured (in capturing PIA documents from HTML, we inadvertently and unavoidable also capture extraneous text, which in this case included a link to "The National DNA Index system" — a reference of the term "DNA" but with no content-based relevance to the PIAs in question).

After discounting for the false positives, we found 12 PIAs discussing federal government systems that include the collection, storage, and dissemination of DNA. One of those PIAs, from the CDC, discusses the collection of "DNA fingerprints" related to food-borne illnesses (in humans); the remainder involves the capture of DNA as PII. Departments with PIAs mentioning the collection/dissemination of DNA include DOJ (the FBI), HHS (CDC, NIH), and DOS. The seven (7) DOS PIAs mention DNA as one type of PII potentially captured by each system. These PIAs do not differentiate between the types of PII captured by each system, so we cannot conclude that these systems necessarily capture DNA as part of their activities, only that it is possible.

Annex I   Example Use and Misuse Cases

I. USE CASES and Mission Needs

- **Federal Aviation Administration**

One of the main functions of the Federal Aviation Administration (FAA) is to monitor and enforce safety issues and policies in all aspects of civil aviation from plane maintenance, pilot health and suitability, runway and facility standards, facility and personnel security, and protection and maintenance of the National Airspace. In order to perform these missions, it is necessary to provide inspectors and special agents with credentialing that mandates immediate access to certain secure areas such as an airliner cockpit or a control tower. There have been occasions where the credentials have been lost or misused for some purpose. Currently, these credentials are not smart enabled.

In the end state, the credentials are tied in with the PIV card Authoritative Database so that if an employee's PIV card is expired, suspended, or revoked, the credential will be as well. The credential will be encoded with biometrics and a certificate(s) to facilitate 'point of presentation' validation. The PIV card itself may become the credential.

In the end state, single sign-on will become a reality with the presentation of a finger on a reader. The sign-on will be available not only for work related systems (network, e-mail, Employee Express, TSP, etc.), but will include public and/or personal sites such as personal email or public sites related to work.

Given the events of 9/11 and the advent of the PIV card, there has been interest in requiring commercial pilot licensees to have PIV type credentials and to go through some sort of identity vetting process that is more rigorous than what now exists. Beyond policy questions about the level of vetting and credential features there are some major logistical issues that emerge. The process of registration is complex. Where would a pilot go to get biometrics taken and to submit proof of identity documents? It is not feasible for the FAA to have personnel at every commercial airport.

In the end state, the applicant pilots, or anyone who needs to prove identity in order to interact with government services, would report to a 'trusted agent' of some sort who would collect biometric and identity proofing information. This data would be processed to the level of vetting deemed necessary for the citizen's requested service and approved by the deliverer of that service.

These are some of the many major issues that need to be addressed:

1. Where does the citizen go to register? Perhaps the trusted agent would be the local post office? A kiosk in a mall?

2. How does the 'trusted agent' submit the application? How does he know where to send it if he is a trusted agent for multiple agencies?

3. How does the citizen receive the credential? Self activation?

- **Department of Defense**

Successful Battlefield Medical Care depends upon several factors, to include accurate baseline knowledge of certain individual physiological qualities, archived since original accession (e.g., blood type, allergies); accurate and timely knowledge of the nature of wounds, injuries or illnesses as they occur; and knowledge of the location and capabilities of medical-response providers and facilities, both in the immediate area, and at more remote locations, depending on the specific need, and progress of treatment.

Knowledge of the medical history of military and other attached government personnel (any of whom can quickly become 'patients'); of the availability, skills, qualifications and locations of medical personnel; and of the facilities where care can be provided, key supplies or medicines located, or specific procedures performed, are all uniquely identifiable and "known."However, these data are archived in disparate data bases and systems, in many locations. While some aspects of identity needed to support healthcare are predictable, such that data can be pre-staged, others are dynamic, and reactive to battlefield conditions that may develop suddenly. Ultimately, the goal of fully-responsive, full-scope medical care remains the same: Be able to access "all" baseline physiology and medical history data, for "all" military personnel, "everywhere" at "all times," and make these available to "all" proper medical responders, wherever located, even as the patient may be moved from place to place to facilitate optimal care…The additional factor of the protections mandated by law relative to personal medical history and records complicates the process by adding requirements for security and accountability to the transmission, storage and use of such private and personal information.

Information-technology networks must be able to access patients, responding practitioners (including remote experts for consultation or telemedicine purposes) and relevant archival data about individuals and medical science. These nets must serve "everybody, everywhere," providing secure, auditable and private information exchange that associates unique individuals and information with accuracy, confidence and efficiency. The unique "identifiability" of all parties to these processes, each within their different roles and privileges, makes this all possible, if the network also possesses all needed capabilities and features to support high-demand, critical identity transactions in complete security.

- **Federal Bureau of Investigation**

Employees of the Federal Bureau of Investigation (FBI) are required to track time, attendance, and leave usage electronically via WebTA. WebTA replaced the FBI's paper-based collection system with a commercial off-the-shelf product providing Bureau employees with an online, Web-based system to record their time and attendance (TA) data. The WebTA system interfaces with several legacy FBI systems and generates an automated interface with the National Finance Center. Although this solution improves the efficiency of the TA process and reduces the overall personnel costs associated with TA, there are still other systems that WebTA could interface with to further stream-line the process. One such system is the stand-alone system that captures arrival times via the PKI access card.

The end state of IdM would enable data sharing between these two stand-alone systems, thereby allowing the automated population of arrival and departure times based on the time employees enter and leave the premises.

Furthermore, multiple systems exist that employees access in the daily performance of their duties. Each of these systems are accessed with user-names and passwords. Passwords are changed periodically for each system. Additionally, there are multiple password requirements for each system, and accounts are frequently suspended due to failed log-on attempts.

The end state of IdM would enable a single sign-on protocol, thereby allowing enterprise network users to seamlessly access all authorized network resources on the basis of a single authentication performed when they initially access the network. This architecture would improve the productivity of network users, reduce the cost of network operations, and improve network security.

- **Federal Trade Commission**

    Employees of the Federal Trade Commission (FTC) are required to have usernames and passwords for numerous unique and independent systems. Employees are required periodically to change their passwords for these various systems. Thus an employee may have as many as eight separate protocols and passwords for the various systems. These systems include the following:

    1. Logging on to the FTC network;

    2. The staff time and activity reporting (STAR) system, where staff record the matters they are working on and the amount of time spent on each;

3. Consumer Sentinel, the FTC's database of consumer complaints;

4. FedTraveler, the government-wide program used to make travel arrangements for employees (administered by a separate agency);

5. Employee Express, used by employees to track their pay and benefits (administered by the Office of Personnel Management);

6. The Thrift Savings Plan (TSP), employees' retirement plan (administered by the Federal Retirement Thrift Investment Board);

7. The Time and Attendance program; and

8. Westlaw and LexisNexis, programs used for legal research.

The end state of IdM should enable a single sign-on protocol. In other words, employees would be able to sign on to the network and have access to all of the systems listed to which they have authorized access, both those administered by the FTC as well as those administered by other agencies. This single sign-on protocol end state system may not be feasible for systems run outside the government, such as Westlaw and LexisNexis.

- **Supply Chain Management**[39]

This topic is not specific to any federal organization, but a matter of general concern. The Government's information technology systems are essential to the successful implementation of electronic identity management. These systems are at increasing risk of supply chain attacks from adversaries enabled by their growing technological sophistication and, more importantly,

---

[39] Excerpted from the Executive Summary of the Committee for National Security Systems. *Framework for Lifecycle Risk Mitigation for National Security Systems in the Era of Globalization.* CNSS Report: 145-06. November 2006, pp ES-1 – ES-3.

facilitated by the rapid globalization of the information technology (IT) marketplace.

Supply chain attacks involve manipulating IT hardware, software, operating systems, peripherals ("IT products"), or services at any point during the life cycle to provide access when the product is delivered to the user. Supply chain attacks are typically conducted or facilitated by individuals or organizations that have access to the products through commercial ties.

Whereas the federal government has traditionally been able to rely on U.S.-based hardware and software suppliers and U.S.-based network operators, globalization is rapidly undermining many of the assumptions concerning supply chain integrity on which we could previously rely. Now, many suppliers are offshore, and even U.S.-based companies use research and manufacturing facilities elsewhere for much of their work. Mergers and acquisitions have changed the ownership and management of many non-government telecommunication and IT infrastructures, placing foreign companies in ultimate control of even domestic operations.

Globalization and its consequences are permanent and irreversible and are likely to have only greater impact over time.

The Defense Science Board's Task Force on *High Performance Chip Supply,* published in February 2005, reported on such trends as they affect only one part of the overall IT industry. The findings exemplify the problem of globalization. One-sixth of the U.S. chip industry no longer has fabrication facilities, and U.S. industry's share of capital expenditures in leading edge semiconductor manufacturing capacity has fallen from 36 percent in 1999 to only 20 percent in 2004.[40] The Task Force concluded, "This [horizontal consolidation of chip fabrication, mask making...] has led to global dispersion of

---

[40] Defense Science Board Task Force, *High Performance Microchip Supply,* February 2005, pp. 19-21.

manufacturing operations, removing many critical operations from U.S. national control."

Moreover, information and telecommunications technologies are quickly converging and, therefore, becoming ever more interconnected—and ever more exposed to potential vulnerabilities. Not only is the changing face of vendors requiring the federal government to rethink its information assurance policies, but also those very telecommunication structures are undergoing fundamental changes affecting how the federal government can design its protective measures.

It is impractical, if not impossible, to avoid the risks of globalization by trying to insulate the federal government from its effects. Instead, there are four identified goals for mitigating risk:

- Enhance the security and resilience of federal government IT and telecommunication infrastructures,

- Identify and mitigate opportunities for exploitation,

- Increase adversaries' cost and risk of exposure, and

- Reduce adversaries' confidence that an attack will be effective.

The traditional approach focuses on protecting the network and attendant infrastructures through layered defenses (e.g., firewalls, intrusion detection systems, public key infrastructure, and cryptography); however, this is not sufficient to mitigate risk arising from increasing globalization and the increasing sophistication of adversaries. Given this reality, any successful strategy must be comprehensive and extend across the product life cycle. It must identify each life cycle phase of a product and also each person or organization with either authorized or possible unauthorized access to the product at each phase where vulnerability could be exploited. An approach that depends too much on protection at one point, or through one evaluation, or from one type of organization, will simply lead adversaries to look elsewhere for a weakness they can exploit. The only way to meet increasing sophistication and globalization is to develop a broad-based response.

To achieve reasonable assurance in the integrity of the supply chain, the risk of vulnerability must be identified, managed, or eliminated at each lifecycle phase listed below.

- Product design and development,
- Manufacturing,
- Packaging,
- Assembly,
- System integration,
- Distribution,
- Operations,
- Maintenance, and
- Retirement.

This comprehensive approach provides a proactive, rather than reactive, strategic framework for lifecycle risk mitigation of supply chain attacks.

- **National Security Screening**

Federal requirements for screening of persons for the purpose of countering terrorism are found in a number of Presidential-level directives, e.g.,:

- Homeland Security Presidential Directive/HSPD-6 ("Integration and Use of Screening Information"). This directive establishes procedures to:

    (1) develop, integrate, and maintain thorough, accurate, and current information about individuals known or appropriately suspected to be or have been engaged in conduct constituting, in preparation for, in aid of, or related to terrorism (Terrorist Information); and

    (2) use that information as appropriate and to the full extent permitted by law to support (a) federal, state, local, territorial, tribal, foreign-government, and private-sector screening processes, and (b) diplomatic, military, intelligence, law enforcement, immigration, visa, and protective processes.

- Homeland Security Presidential Directive/HSPD-11 ("Comprehensive Terrorist-Related Screening Procedures"). This directive seeks to:

    (1) Enhance terrorist-related screening…through comprehensive, coordinated procedures that detect, identify, track, and interdict

people, cargo, conveyances, and other entities and objects that pose a threat to homeland security, and to do so in a manner that safeguards legal rights, including freedoms, civil liberties, and information privacy guaranteed by federal law, and builds upon existing risk assessment capabilities while facilitating the efficient movement of people, cargo, conveyances, and other potentially affected activities in commerce; and

(2) Implement a coordinated and comprehensive approach to terrorist-related screening — in immigration, law enforcement, intelligence, counterintelligence, and protection of the border, transportation systems, and critical infrastructure — that supports homeland security, at home and abroad.

These directives are readily accessible and may be studied in full. However, detailed procedures regarding the actual conduct of screening operations are generally too sensitive to be included in this report.

- **Department of State**

The Department of State is responsible for the worldwide diplomatic mission for the United States. In this role, the Department operates a global information technology (IT) infrastructure that must provide confidentiality and integrity, while operating at a high level of availability. In order to perform its mission, the Department must be able to easily and securely access a wide range of data and materials on the Sensitive but Unclassified network. Strong authentication protocols ensure that this mandate is feasible and that sensitive data is properly protected. The Department's Public Key Infrastructure (PKI) and associated biometric logon capability provide enhanced levels of security and user authentication to this critical, global network.

The Department implemented its first PKI over half a decade ago. That PKI provided the platform on which other PKIs have been built, providing a constantly widening range of features and security. The current functionality is very broad. A PKI on the Active Directory based network (the AD PKI) that enables both encryption and digital signature for users at the desktop level is currently available. This same PKI provides the ability for the Department to sign mobile code and provides an infrastructure to enable a high-assurance logon process for applications. The PIV PKI currently provides certificates that can be used in the authentication process with other government agencies. Further, the Machine Readable Travel Document (MRTD) PKI provides the infrastructure that enables the digital signing of data on the new electronic passports.

Coupled to the AD PKI is the use of integrated biometrics for user authentication. This sophisticated process uses match-on-card technology, which provides one-to-one matching of the minutia on the smart ID to the fingerprint presented by the user. Such a process eliminates the network latency associated with a one-to-many match in a network database, both enhancing logon speed and significantly improving the security of the biometric. Besides the higher level of assurance associated with a biometric logon, this process also eliminates the need to remember passwords for system logon. Applications that are integrated can also use the same biometric logon, further enhancing the ease of use for users and improving network security. This is a win for all.

Unfortunately, full deployment of both PKI and biometrics has been delayed due to budget constraints. Consequently, this technology has not yet matured in the Department in terms of broad acceptance and use. The end state for the Department should include a complete deployment of PKI and biometric logon capabilities to all desktops. This final level of deployment would enable security functionality such as full digital signing of all e-mail traffic. It would also provide single sign-on for a wide range of applications, further enhancing and securing the network environment. The ultimate elimination of numerous complex passwords will certainly make users happier and eliminate the typical security holes that invariably exist with passwords.

- **National Science Foundation**

The National Science Foundation conducts about 5000 meetings each year to evaluate proposals for research and education. Each of these meetings occupies the time of 10 to 20 outside subject matter experts (who we call reviewers) for 1 to 3 days. Of course, the success of the meetings depends greatly on who we invite, and their willingness to attend depends on their past experiences. Since our reviewer pool is our most valuable resource for distinguishing high-quality projects, we try to ensure a positive experience for every reviewer every time.

Reviewer recruitment and management is currently a multistep process:

1. Currently a program director will start with an idea of the subject matter expertise required for a particular review meeting, and will search for reviewers using a combination of internal and external databases.

2. Having found a reviewer, the program director makes initial contact with the reviewer to determine availability and interest, then passes the names of available reviewers to a program assistant.

3. The program assistant checks the names for membership in our internal reviewer database, and contacts those reviewers who are new to our database for addresses, phone numbers, email addresses, and other information.

4. Once the meeting roster is complete the program assistant prepares group travel orders and sends email to the reviewers with instructions for arranging travel.

5. Meanwhile, the program director sends a list of proposals to be reviewed and review instructions to each reviewer. The program director also asks each reviewer to note any existing relationships that might pose ethical problems in evaluating proposals. The program director and program assistant set up an electronic reviewing system to be used on the day of the meeting, specifying the role of each reviewer with regard to each proposal.

6. Reviewers arrange their own travel using FedTraveller. NSF staff stands by to help.

7. On the day of the meeting, reviewers sign in and conduct business using the electronic reviewing system. They must at this time fill out a direct-deposit form and give us their SSNs so that we can reimburse their expenses and pay a consulting fee.

8. Once the meeting is over, information on the reviewers is sent to our financial division which begins arranging payment.

9. The program director notes the performance and expertise of each reviewer to aid in organizing later meetings. This information may be kept privately or (rarely) may be entered into the NSF internal review database.

10. Two to six weeks after reviewers return home most are reimbursed. Those that are not or who have some problems get in touch with the program director and assistant, who work with other parts of NSF to resolve the issues.

11. Several months after the meeting, issues have been resolved and all reviewers have been paid.

Several of the steps above could be simplified or eliminated in the end state of identity management. If a reviewer has served NSF before, there is no need to collect redundant information, eliminating steps 3, part of 7, 8, and 11. We could have the travel system suggest an itinerary and hotel based on past choices, eliminating step 6. We could eliminate the multiple entries into our silos and greatly reduce the errors that arise from transferring information manually between systems. If this reviewer process were integrated with our proposal and award process, we could automate other aspects of this work, for example by finding reviewers who currently had projects ongoing that were similar to the one proposed, easing step 1.

II. MISUSE CASES – Activities and behaviors to be detected and prevented.

- **Disclosure of identifier information**. The IdM system could improperly disclose identifier information to a third party. This may be carried out by a man-in-the-middle attack, where a malefactor inserts itself into the communication path between a user and the system, spoofs messages both ways, and captures information intended for the system. It may be carried out by spyware or other malware inserted into the user's computer or into the IdM server. It may be carried out by social engineering, in which a malefactor convinces a human involved with the IdM system to disclose information, perhaps under a pretense of a forgotten password.

- **Use of disclosed identifier information**. Once disclosed, the identifier information can be used improperly. This could be used to gather further information on the user, to change information about the user, to deny access to the user, or to spoof interactions with either people or IdM systems in the federation.

- **Identifier information held by adversaries and partners**. Other entities will hold information on U.S. persons, and could use that information to improperly access U.S. IdM systems. This could come from entry records into foreign countries, from purchased credit bureau reports, or from separate IdM systems that collect the same information as the U.S. ones. It is conceivable that a trusted partner could in the future become an adversary and misuse information that had been shared during the partnership. A partner might have a less secure IdM system than the government, in which case information might be disclosed by the partner.

Annex J International Standards Organizations Involved in IdM

In the area of technical IdM standards to achieve global interoperability, two of the most active are the International Telecommunication Union (ITU) and the International Organization for Standardization (ISO). In the area of developing non-technical IdM policies, the Organization for Economic Co-operation and Development (OECD) has begun to play a role. It should be noted that in addition to these organizations, there are several commercial efforts underway to develop IdM standards. However, because this report is focused on the federal government scope cited at the outset, the various commercial IdM initiatives are not addressed. The only exception is the ISO, discussed below, where there is significant federal participation.

The International Telecommunication Union. The International Telecommunication Union (ITU) is a UN agency that is distinguished from other standards development organizations by the fact that its membership formally includes both national administrations and the private sector. There are currently about 191 Member States and more than 700 private sector members in the ITU. The ITU is organized into a Radiocommunication Sector (ITU-R), a Telecommunication Sector (ITU-T), and a Development Sector (ITU-D). The ITU-T has several IdM standards (known as Recommendations) under development, and has recently completed development of a Recommendation on "Requirements for global identity management trust and interoperability," X.1250. This recommendation is now in the process of being approved by ITU members.

X.1250 provides a structured set of requirements for capabilities necessary for global IdM trust and interoperability, i.e., to enable known trust in the assertions about digital identities (credentials, identifiers, attributes and reputations) used in all communication and control networks and services. It will be in the ITU-T approval process until September 2008. It is the first global intergovernmental-industry standard of its kind, and provides the core definitions and framework for all subsequent ITU-T IdM recommendations.

A structured set of requirements for capabilities necessary for global IdM trust and interoperability is essential to enable known trust in the assertions about digital identities (credentials, identifiers, attributes and reputations) used in all communication and control networks and services. The use of the term "global" here refers to both worldwide geography, as well as applicability to the entire array of telecommunication/ICT networks and services.

The implementation of IdM among governmental and private-sector networks and services will remain very diverse, highly distributed, substantially autonomous, and constantly evolving. This dynamic diversity was a consideration in defining these requirements. The specification includes available references to best practices for the protection of personally identifiable information.

The specification comprises nine sections of essential requirements:

1. **A common identity management model**.
2. **An interoperable set of IdM functions**.
3. **Establishes four basic Identity Services:** credential, identifier, attribute, and reputation identity services with known assurance levels to all entities.
4. **Discovery of authoritative identity provider resources, services, and Federations**.
5. **Interoperability and bridging**.
6. **Security and policy**.
7. **Auditing and compliance**.
8. **Performance, reliability, availability**.
9. **Internationalization**.

As noted, this standard has not been finally adopted by the entire international community, and the U.S. government will need to carefully study the adoption of its precepts, in consideration of the complexity of the current IdM architecture and future needs. In any case, it is clear at the outset that the emergence of this proposal represents a pivotal development in the progress of global IdM, inasmuch as it represents the topic in a truly universal way, for the first time, across the international community.

The International Organization for Standardization (ISO). The ISO is the world's largest standards development organization. Although its membership is organized along national lines, member states are represented by national standards bodies referred to as technical advisory groups. The American National Standards Institute (ANSI) is the United States technical advisory group to ISO.

ISO's standardization program covers a wide variety of subjects, including Information Technology. The Information Technology work is under the auspices of Joint Technical Committee One (JTC1) for which ANSI serves as Secretariat. JTC1 has a number of subcommittees addressing telecommunications and IdM. Among other subcommittees, the following three should be of interest to any federal government IdM undertaking.

- ISO/IEC JTC 1 Sub Committee 17 — Responsible for all identification cards and related interface and device standards.

- ISO/IEC JTC 1 Sub Committee 27 — ,Responsible for security and privacy technology standards.

- ISO/IEC JTC 1 Sub Committee 37 — Responsible for biometric standards

It is customary for ISO and ITU-T to coordinate the preparation and publication of documents where there is sufficient common interest and work.

The Organization for Economic Co-operation and Development. In the multilateral context, one organization that develops non-technical policies is the OECD. The OECD is a forum in which the governments of thirty member countries (including the United States) address the economic, social, environmental, and governance challenges and opportunities of the globalizing world economy. Non-members such as business, civil society, and other international organizations also attend and provide input and advice. One of the OECD committees is the Committee for Information, Computer and Communications Policy (ICCP). The Working Party on Information Security and Privacy (WPISP) is a subgroup that works under the ICCP's direction. The WPISP's terms of reference include the following:

"To monitor and analyze developments and trends in security of information systems and networks, and protection of personal data and privacy in the Digital Economy/Global information society and to develop and propose policy options for security of information systems and networks, and protection of personal data and privacy."

Annex K Identity Management Glossary

This glossary is largely copied from the one adapted and used in the development of the ITU's IdM standards. It was selected for the TF's purposes due to its currency, international and government/industry scope, and generally comprehensive nature. Even so, the TF did add a few terms, as used or adapted herein. Also, two definitions were changed to conform to current federal standards: "Biometrics," as used in the NSTC Subcommittee on Biometrics and Identity Management, inter alia; and "PII," as used by the Office of Management and Budget.

Term	Definition(s)
access control	The prevention of unauthorized use of a resource, including the prevention of use of a resource in an unauthorized manner.
address	An address is the identifier for a specific termination point and is used for routing to this termination point.
agent	A computer system or device that has been delegated (authority, responsibility, a function, etc.) by and acts for a Party (in exercising the authority, carrying out the responsibility, performing the function, etc.).
alliance	An agreement between two or more independent Entities that defines how they will relate to each other and how they jointly conduct activities.
anonymity	i. *Ability to allow anonymous access to services, which avoid tracking of user's personal information and user behaviour such as user location, frequency of a service usage, and so on.* ii. Lack of any capability to ascertain identity. iii. The quality or state of being anonymous, which is the condition of having a name or identity that is unknown or concealed.
assertion	i. **A representation of an entity's identity or claim**. (Compare with manifestation.) ii. The identity information provided by an Identity Provider to a Service Provider.
asserting identity	An entity making an identity representation or claim to a relying party within some request context.

Term	Definition(s)
asset	Anything that has value to the organization, its business, its operations and its continuity.
assurance (or at least authentication assurance)	A measure of confidence that the security features and architecture of the Identity Management capabilities accurately mediate and enforce the security policies understood between the Relying Party and the Identity Provider.
assurance level	A quantitative expression of Assurance agreed between a Relying Party and an Identity Provider.
asymmetric authentication method	A method of authentication, in which not all authentication information is shared by both entities.
attribute	*i. Descriptive information bound to an entity that specifies a characteristic of an entity such as condition, quality or other information associated with that entity* ii. Information of a particular type. In the IdM, objects and object classes are composed of attributes. iii. A distinct characteristic of an object. An object's attributes are said to describe the object. Objects' attributes are often specified in terms of their physical traits, such as size, shape, weight, and color, etc., for real-world objects. Objects in cyberspace might have attributes describing size, type of encoding, network address, etc.
attribute type	That component of an attribute which indicates the class of information given by that attribute.
attribute value	A particular instance of the class of information indicated by an attribute type.
audit (secret)	An independent review and examination of system records and activities in order to test for adequacy of system controls, to ensure compliance with established policy and operational procedures, to detect breaches in security, and to recommend any indicated changes in control, policy and procedures.
authenticated identity	A distinguishing identifier of a principal that has been assured through authentication.
authentication	The provision of assurance of the claimed identity of an entity.
authentication certificate	A security certificate that is guaranteed by an authentication authority and that may be used to assure the identity of an entity.
authentication exchange	A sequence of one or more transfers of exchange authentication information (AI) for the purposes of performing an authentication.

Term	Definition(s)
authentication information	*i.* ***Information used to establish the validity of a claimed identity.*** ii. Information used for authentication purposes.
authentication initiator	The entity that starts an authentication exchange.
authorization	The granting of rights, which includes the granting of access based on access rights.
authoritative identity provider	The Identity Provider responsible by law, industry practice, or system implementation for the definitive identity response to a query.
binding	An explicit established association, bonding, or tie.
biometrics	A general term used alternatively to describe a characteristic or a process. *As a characteristic*: A measurable biological (anatomical and physiological) and behavioral characteristic that can be used for automated recognition. *As a process*: Automated methods of recognizing an individual based on measurable biological (anatomical and physiological) and behavioral characteristics.
certificate (secret)	A set of security-relevant data issued by a security authority or a trusted third party, together with security information which is used to provide the integrity and data origin authentication services for the data.
circle of trust	*i.* ***A set of criteria established for joining organizations within a federation for the purposes of trusted access to each other's resources*** ii. Federation of service providers and identity providers that have business relationships based on Liberty architecture, and operational agreements, with whom users can transact business in a secure and seamless environment.
claim	An assertion made by a Claimant of the value or values of one or more Identity Attributes of a Digital Subject, typically an assertion which is disputed or in doubt.
claimant	*i.* **An entity which is or represents a principal for the purposes of authentication. A claimant includes the functions necessary for engaging in authentication exchanges on behalf of a principal**. ii. A Digital Subject representing a Party that makes a Claim.

Term	Definition(s)
claim authentication information	Information used by a claimant to generate exchange AI needed to authenticate a principal.
context	A property that can be associated with a user attribute value to specify information that can be used to determine the applicability of the value.
credential	*i. An identifiable object that can be used to authenticate the claimant is what it claims to be and authorize the claimant's access rights* ii. Data that is transferred to establish the claimed identity of an entity. iii. The private part of a paired Identity assertion (user-id is usually the public part). The thing(s) that an Entity relies upon in an Assertion at any particular time, usually to authenticate a claimed Identity. Credentials can change over time and may be revoked. Examples include; a signature, a password, a drivers licence number (not the card itself), an ATM card number (not the card itself), data stored on a smart-card (not the card itself), a digital certificate, a biometric template.
data origin authentication	Corroboration that the source of data received is as claimed.
delegation	*i. Conveyance of privilege from one entity that holds such privilege, to another entity.* ii. The action that assigns authority, responsibility or a function to another object. iii. An act of transferring of privileges to perform some action on behalf of one entity to another.
digital contract	A contract made in digital form and signed by two entities between whom an agreement is reached.
digital identity	i. *The digital representation of the information known about a specific individual, group or organization* ii. A digital representation of a set of Claims made by one Party about itself or another Digital Subject. iii. A set of claims made by one digital subject about itself or another digital subject.
digital identity provider	An Agent that issues a Digital Identity.
digital subject	An Entity represented or existing in the digital realm which is being described or dealt with.
directed identity	A unifying identity system must support both "omni-directional" identifiers for public entities and "unidirectional"

Term	Definition(s)
	identifiers for private entities.
discovery	i. *The act of locating a machine-processable description of a network-related resource that may have been previously unknown and that meets certain functional criteria. It involves matching a set of functional and other criteria with a set of resource descriptions. The goal is to find an appropriate Web service-related resource.* ii. The process by which IdM resources can be found or located.
electronic identity	The information about a registered entity that the Identity Provider has chosen to represent the Identity of that entity. The eID includes a name or an identifier for the entity that is unique within the domain of the Identity Provider.
enrolment	The enrolment of an entity is the process in which the entity is identified and/or other attributes are corroborated.
entity	i. *Anything that has separate and distinct existence that can be uniquely identified. In the context of IdM, examples of entities include subscribers, users, network elements, networks, software applications, services and devices. An entity may have multiple identifiers.* ii. An entity is anyone (natural or legal person) or anything that shall be characterised through the measurement of its attributes. iii. A person, physical object, animal, or juridical entity. iv. A particular thing, such as a person, place, process, object, concept, association, or event.
federation	i. *An act of establishing a relationship between two or more entities or an association compromising any number of service providers and identity providers* ii. An established relationship among a domain of a single service provider or among NGN providers. iii. A federation is a collection of realms that have established a producer-consumer relationship whereby one realm can provide authorized access to a resource it manages based on an identity, and possibly associated attributes, that are asserted in another realm. A federation requires trust such that a Relying Party can make a well-informed access control decision based on the credibility of identity and attribute data that is vouched for by another realm.
federated identity	i. *A collective term describing agreements standards and technologies that make identity and entitlements portable across autonomous domains* ii. A single user identity that can be used to access a group

Term	Definition(s)
	of services or applications that are bounded by the ties and conditions of a federation. **iii.** A shared Identity and/or authentication, as the result of federation by either the Entity or by two or more organisations.
identification	The process of verifying the identity of a user, process, or device, usually as a prerequisite for granting access to resources in an IT system.
identification services	Services that aggregate an entity's identities to provide trust levels in the bindings between those identities and the entity.
identifier	**i.** *An identifier is a series of digits, characters and symbols or any other form of data used to identify subscriber(s), user(s), network element(s), function(s), network entity(ies) providing services/applications, or other entities (e.g., physical or logical objects).* **ii.** A data object (for example, a string) mapped to a system entity that uniquely refers to the system entity. A system entity may have multiple distinct identifiers referring to it. An identifier is essentially a "distinguished attribute" of an entity. **iii.** Either an "http" or "https" URI, (commonly referred to as a "URL" within this document), or an XRI (Reed, D. and D. McAlpin, "Extensible Resource Identifier (XRI) Syntax V2.0,".) **iv.** Strings or tokens that are unique within a given scope (globally or locally within a specific domain, community, directory, application, etc.). Identifiers are the key used by the parties to an identification relationship to agree on the entity being represented. Identifiers may be classified as omnidirectional and unidirectional. Omnidirectional identifiers are intended to be public and easily discoverable, while unidirectional identifiers are intended to be private and used only in the context of a specific identity relationship. Identifiers may also be classified as resolvable or non-resolvable. Resolvable identifiers, such as a domain name or e-mail address, may be dereferenced into the entity they represent. Non-resolvable identifiers, such as a person's real-world name, or a subject or topic name, can be compared for equivalence but are not otherwise machine-understandable. There are many different schemes and formats for digital identifiers. The most widely used is Uniform Resource Identifier (URI) and its internationalized version Internationalized Resource Identifier (IRI)—the standard for identifiers on the World Wide Web. OpenID and Light-Weight Identity (LID) are two web authentication protocols that use standard HTTP URIs (often

Term	Definition(s)
	called URLs), for example. A new OASIS standard for abstract, structured identifiers, XRI (Extensible Resource Identifiers), adds new features to URIs and IRIs that are especially useful for digital identity systems. OpenID **v.** An attribute or a set of attributes of an entity which uniquely identifies the entity within a certain context. (For the sake of clarity, identifiers consisting of one attribute are also characteristics; they distinguish an entity from other entities. An entity may have multiple distinct identifiers referring to it. Identifiers uniquely identify an entity, while characteristics do not need to. However, it should be noted that identifiers can consist of a combination of attributes, whereas characteristics are always one single attribute.)
identity	**i. Structured representations of an entity in the form of one or more credentials, identifiers, attributes, or patterns in a relevant context. Such representations can take any physical or electro-optical (digital or analog) form or syntax, and may have associated implicit or explicit time-stamp and location specifications.** **ii.** The properties of an entity that allows it to be distinguished from other entities. **iii.** The attributes by which an entity is described, recognized or known. **iv.** The essence of an entity and often described by its characteristics. **v.** The essence of an entity [Merriam]. One's identity is often described by one's characteristics, among which may be any number of identifiers. **vi.** The fundamental concept of uniquely identifying an object (person, computer, etc.) within a context. That context might be local (within a department), corporate (within an enterprise), national (within the bounds of a country), global (all such object instances on the planet), and possibly universal (extensible to environments not yet known). Many identities exist for local, corporate, and national domains. Some globally unique identifiers exist for technical environments, often computer-generated. **vii.** A collection of attributes which helps to distinguish one entity from another.
identity agent	Manages and supports a consistent user experience (and in some cases other kinds of interactions) with a Service Provider.
identity attribute	A property of a Digital Subject that may have zero or more values.

Term	Definition(s)
identity based security policy	A security policy based on the identities and/or attributes of users, a group of users, or entities acting on behalf of the users and the resources/objects being accessed.
identity bridge provider	An Identity Provider that acts as a trusted intermediary among other Identity Providers.
identity context	The surrounding environment and circumstances that determine meaning of Digital Identities and the policies and protocols that govern their interactions.
identity information	All the information identifying a user, including trusted (network generated) and/or untrusted (user generated) addresses. Identity information shall take the form of either a SIP URI (see <u>RFC 2396</u>) or a "tel" URI (see <u>RFC 3966</u>).
identity defederation	The action occurring when Providers agree to stop referring to an entity via a certain set of identifiers and/or attributes.
identity federation	The act of creating a federated identity on behalf of an entity.
identity layer	A common layer where identity information can be exchanged between different systems.
identity management	The combination of technical systems, rules and procedures that define the ownership, utilization, and safeguard of personal identity information. The primary goal of the Identity Management process is to assign attributes to a digital identity, and to connect that identity to an individual.
identity pattern	A structured expression derived from the behaviour of an entity that contributes to the recognition process; this may include the reputation of the entity. Identity patterns may be uniquely associated with an entity, or a class with which the entity is associated.
identity proofing	A shareable, identity management component by which the credential issuer validates sufficient information to uniquely identify a person applying for the credential.
identity provider	**i.** *An entity that creates, maintains, and manages trusted identity information for entities. An Identity Provider may include a Trusted Third Party as well as Relying Parties and entities themselves in different contexts.* **ii.** A type of service provider that creates, maintains, and manages identity information for users/devices and provides user/device authentication. **iii.** A service provider that authenticates a user and that creates, maintains, and manages identity information for users and asserts user authentication and other identity related information to other trusted service providers.

Term	Definition(s)
	iv. An entity in an AAI that performs Identity Management. **v.** Kind of service provider that creates, maintains, and manages identity information for principals and provides authentication to other service providers within a federation, such as with web browser profiles.
identity registration	The process of making a person's identity known to the (Personal Identity Verification) system, associating a unique identifier with that identity, and collecting and recording the person's relevant attributes into the system.
identity verification	The process of affirming that a claimed identity is correct by comparing the offered claims of identity with previously proven information.
internationalization	The process of planning and implementing Identity Management specifications, products, services, and administrative implementations so that they can easily be adapted to specific local technical platforms, languages, and cultures, a process called localization.
interoperability	The ability of independent systems to exchange meaningful information and initiate actions from each other, in order to operate together to mutual benefit. In particular, it envisages the ability for loosely-coupled independent systems to be able to collaborate and communicate; the possibility of use in services outside the direct control of the issuing assigner.
layer network	A "topological component" that represents the complete set of access groups of the same type which may be associated for the purpose of transferring information.
manifestation	An observed or discovered (i.e., not self-asserted) representation of an entity's identity or claim. (Compare with assertion.)
mutual authentication	Requirement that both the service provider and the user identify each other.
data	A relationship that someone claims to exist between two entities.
name	A name is the identifier of an entity (e.g., subscriber, network element) that may be resolved/translated into an address.
network transparency	The ability of a protocol to transmit data over the network in a manner which is transparent to those using the applications that are using the protocol.
non-repudiation	**i.** *The ability to prove an action or event has taken place, so that this event or action cannot be repudiated later*

Term	Definition(s)
	ii. The ability through historical logs and logical analysis to prevent or discourage an Entity from denying that it had acted as an Identity in a given transaction, especially in a legal sense.
object	**i.** *A well-defined piece of information, definition, or specification which requires a name in order to identify its use in an instance of communication <u>and identity management processing.</u>* **ii.** Entity within the scope of the DOI system; the entity may be abstract, physical or digital, as any of these forms of entity may be of relevance in content management (e.g., people, resources, agreements).
owner	The registered Entity for an Identity.
party	A natural person or a legal entity.
path layer network	A "layer network" which is independent of the transmission media and which is concerned with the transfer of information between path layer network "access points."
peer-entity authentication	The corroboration that a peer entity in an association is the one claimed.
persistent	Existing, and able to be used in services outside the direct control of the issuing assigner, without a stated time limit.
personally identifiable information (PII)	**i.** The information pertaining to any person which makes it possible to identify such individual (including the information capable of identifying a person when combined with other information even if the information does not clearly identify the person). Note: Information that can be used to identify an individual should be defined by national legislation. **ii.** Any information which identifies a person to any degree.
policy	A set of Rules, usually associated with a Role or other dynamic attributes.
presence	**i.** A set of attributes that characterize an entity (maintained by a "presentity") relating to current activity, environment, geolocation, communication means and contact addresses. **ii.** A set of data representing the status and availability of a user or a group of users for communication.
presentity (presence entity)	An entity that makes presence information available for use by others.

Term	Definition(s)
	Any uniquely identifiable entity that is capable of providing presence information to presence service. Examples of presentities are devices, services etc.
principal	An entity whose identity can be authenticated.
privacy	**i.** ***The right of entities to control or influence what information related to them may be collected and stored also by whom and to whom that information may be disclosed.*** **ii.** Ensuring that information about a person is protected in accordance with national, regional, or global regulations. Such information may be contained within a message, but may also be inferred from patterns of communication; e.g., when communications happen, the types of resource accessed, the parties with whom communication occurs, etc. **iii.** A right to control the dissemination of the attributes of an entity. **iv.** The rights and limitations of access to and processing of personal data. **v.** Proper handling of personal information throughout its life cycle, consistent with the preferences of the subject.
privacy policy	**i.** ***The policy statement that defines the rules for protecting access to and dissemination of personal privacy information*** **ii.** A set of rules and practices that specify or regulate how a person or organization collects, processes (uses) and discloses another party's personal data as a result of an interaction.
private (subscriber) identity	An identity derived from the IMSI.
private identifier	A Claimed Identifier that is intended to be private information used only the context of the End User's relationship with one or more specific Relying Parties (typically one or a small number). The use of Private Identifiers reduces or eliminates the ability of multiple Relying Parties to do correlation of an End User.
Privilege	**i.** ***A right to carry out a particular permission (act) that is assigned to a role with some constraints or conditions. A role is (can be) associated with multiple privileges.*** **ii.** An attribute or property assigned to an entity by an authority. **iii.** An authorization or set of authorizations to perform security-relevant functions.
proofing	The verification or validation of information when enrolling

Term	Definition(s)
	new entities into identity systems.
provisioning	Automatically providing an Identity with access to a role, resource or service, or automatically changing or removing that access, based on the life cycle of events or work requests or changed attributes.
pseudonym	A fictitious identity that an Entity creates for itself, whereby the Entity can remain pseudonymous, or perhaps even fully anonymous, in certain contexts.
public (subscriber) identity	Either a SIP URI or a tel URI.
public service identifier	Either a SIP URI or a tel URI.
quality of assurance	See "assurance level."
relying party	**i.** **An entity that relies on an identity representation or claim by a Requesting/ Asserting entity within some request context.** **ii.** A user or agent that relies on the data in a certificate in making decisions. **iii.** A Party that makes known through its Agent one or more alternative sets of Claims that it desires or requires, and receives through this same Agent a Digital Identity purportedly including the required Claims from a Digital Identity Provider or other Agent of another Party. **iv.** The entity that relies on the result of an authentication. Usually, but not always, the same as the authenticating party and service provider. **v.** Recipient of a certificate who acts in reliance on that certificate and/or digital signatures verified using that certificate (see IETF RFC 3647). **vi.** The recipient of a message that relies on a request message and associated assertions to determine whether to provide a requested service.
repudiation	**i.** *Denial by one of the entities involved in a communication of having participated in all or part of the communication* **ii.** An ability to provide public notice that identity credentials, identifiers, attributes, or patterns have been revoked or not valid. **iii.** An entity involved in a communication exchange subsequently denies the fact.
requesting entity	An Entity making an identity representation or claim to a relying party within some request context.

Term	Definition(s)
revocation	The act (by someone having the authority) of annulling something previously done.
role	*A set of properties or attributes that describes the capabilities of an entity that can be performed. An activity performed by an entity; each entity can play many roles.* A position or function of an organization that describes the authority and responsibility conferred on an entity assigned to the role.
security domain	A set of elements, a security policy, a security authority and a set of security-relevant activities in which the elements are managed in accordance with the security policy. The policy will be administered by the security authority. A given security domain may span multiple security zones.
security zone	A protected area. This is defined by operational control, location, and connectivity to other device/network elements.
security domain authority	A security authority that is responsible for the implementation of a security policy for a security domain.
self-asserted identity	An identity asserted by an entity itself.
service	A set of functions and facilities offered to a user by a provider.
symmetric authentication method	A method of authentication in which both entities share common authentication information.
terminal object	An object having a binding to a terminal device, such as a Subscriber Identity Module (SIM) card.
trail	A "transport entity" which consists of an associated pair of "unidirectional trails" capable of simultaneously transferring information in opposite directions between their respective inputs and outputs.
transmission media layer network	A "layer network" which may be media dependent and which is concerned with the transfer of information between transmission media layer network "access points" in support of one or more "path layer networks."
transport	The functional process of transferring information between different locations.
transport entity	An architectural component which transfers information between its inputs and outputs within a layer network.
transport network	The functional resources of the network which conveys user information between locations.
trust	i. A measure of reliance on the character, ability, strength, or truth of someone or something.

Term	Definition(s)
	ii. Confidence that an entity will behave in a particular way with respect to certain activities (entity X is said to trust entity Y for a set of activities if and only if entity X relies upon entity Y behaving in a particular way with respect to the activities.) iii. A reasonable level of confidence that an entity will behave in a certain manner in a given context. iv. A subjective assessment. An instance of a relationship between two or more entities, in which an entity assumes that another entity will act as authorised/expected. v. Trust is an evaluation, by an entity, of the reliability of an identity when the identity is involved in interactions.
trust level	A consistent, quantifiable measure of reliance on the character, ability, strength, or truth of someone or something.
trusted but vulnerable zone	From the viewpoint of a NGN provider a security zone where the network elements/devices are operated (provisioned and maintained) by the NGN provider. The equipment may be under the control by either the customer/subscriber or the NGN provider. In addition, the equipment may be located within or outside the NGN provider's domain. They communicate with elements both in the trusted zone and with elements in the un-trusted zone, which is why they are "vulnerable." Their major security function is to protect the NEs in the trusted zone from the security attacks originated in the un-trusted zone in a fail-safe manner.
trusted entity	An entity that can violate a security policy, either by performing actions which it is not supposed to do, or by failing to perform actions which it is supposed to do.
trusted identity information	Network-generated user public identity information.
trusted third party	A security authority or its agent that is trusted with respect to some security relevant activities (in the context of a security policy).
trusted zone	From the viewpoint of a NGN provider a security domain where a NGN provider's network elements and systems reside and never communicate directly with customer equipment. The common characteristics of NGN network elements in this domain are that they are under the full control of the related NGN provider, are located in the NGN provider premises (which provides physical security), and they communicate only with elements in the "trusted" domain and with elements in the "trusted-but-vulnerable" domain.
untrusted zone	From the viewpoint of a NGN provider a zone that includes

Term	Definition(s)
	all network elements of customer networks or possibly peer networks or other NGN provider zones outside of the original domain, which are connected to the NGN provider's border elements.
user	i. *Includes end user, person, subscriber, system, equipment, terminal (e.g., FAX, PC), (functional) entity, process, application, provider, or corporate network.* ii. An Identity where the identifier of the identity is the public part of a paired Identity assertion.
user identifiers	Identifiers that represent users in their interactions with other parties. Users may present their identifiers verbally, on paper, on plastic cards, or in any other appropriate manner. Electronic user identifiers are electronically presented over data communication channels by user-operated computing devices (client devices) such as PCs, laptops, mobile phones, and smartcards.
user identity	A code or string uniquely identifying a user across a multi-user, multi-service infrastructure.
verification	The process of confirming a claimed Identity. For example; any one-to-one precise matching of an identity's registered credentials, such as in a logon or any non-AFIS process. Usually performed in real-time, with a yes/no outcome.
verification authentication information (verification AI)	Information used by a verifier to verify an identity claimed through exchange AI.
verifier	An entity that is or represents the entity requiring an authenticated identity. A verifier includes the functions necessary for engaging in authentication exchanges.

Annex L Bibliography

Cameron, K. (2006, Jan. 9, 2006). Laws of Identity in Brief. Retrieved June 20, 2008, from http://www.identityblog.com/?p=353

Defense Science Board Task Force. (2007). *Report on Defense Biometrics*. Washington, DC: Office of the Under Secretary of Defense for Acquisition, Technology, and Logistics. http://www.acq.osd.mil/dsb/reports/2007-03-Biometrics.pdf

Federal Trade Commission. (2003). *Identity Theft Survey Report*. Washington, DC: Federal Trade Commission. http://www.ftc.gov/os/2007/11/SynovateFinalReportIDTheft2006.pdf

Graeff, T. R., and Harmon, S. (2002). Collecting and using personal data: consumers' awareness and concerns. *Journal of Consumer Marketing, 19*(4), 302-318.

Hammond, W. E. (1997). The Use of Social Security Number as the Basis for a National Citizen Identifier. In Computer Science and Telecommunications Board (Ed.), *The Unpredictable Certainty: White Papers*. Washington, DC: The National Academies Press.

Homeland Security Presidential Directive 6, (2003) http://www.whitehouse.gov/news/releases/2003/09/20030916-5.html

Homeland Security Presidential Directive 11, (2004) http://www.whitehouse.gov/news/releases/2004/08/20040827-7.html

Homeland Security Presidential Directive 12, (2004). http://www.whitehouse.gov/news/releases/2004/08/20040827-8.html

International Biometric Group. (2005). *Independent Testing of Iris Recognition Technology*. New York.

Kent, S. T., and Millett, L. I. (Eds.). (2003). *Who Goes There?: Authentication Through the Lens of Privacy*. Washington, DC: The National Academies Press.

Klingenstein, N. (2007, 04/2007). *Attribute Aggregation and Federated Identity*. Paper presented at the International Symposium on Applications and the Internet Workshops (SAINTW)

Lafky, D. B. (2008). Representing The People: An Ontological Approach to Managing Identity in e-Government Applications. *In review*.

Lewis, J. A. (2008). *Authentication 2.0: New Opportunities for Online Identification*. Washington, DC: Center for Strategic and International Studies. http://www.csis.org/media/csis/pubs/080115_authentication.pdf

London School of Economics: The Department of Information Systems. (2005). *The Identity Project: An assessment of the UK Identity Cards Bill and its implications*. London: London School of Economics and Political Science. http://eprints.lse.ac.uk/741/1/PressRelease_5-09-05.pdf

National Science and Technology Council, Committee on Technology, Committee on Homeland and National Security, and Subcommittee on Biometrics. (2006). *Privacy & Biometrics: Building a Conceptual Foundation*. Washington, DC: National Science and Technology Council. http://www.biometrics.gov/docs/privacy.pdf

National Science and Technology Council Subcommittee on Biometrics. (2006). *The National Biometrics Challenge*. Washington, DC: National Science and Technology Council. http://www.biometrics.gov/Documents/biochallengedoc.pdf

National Science and Technology Council Subcommittee on Biometrics. (2007). *NSTC Policy for Enabling the Development, Adoption, and Use of Biometric Standards*. Washington, DC: National Science and Technology Council. http://www.biometrics.gov/Standards/NSTC_Policy_Bio_Standards.pdf

National Security Presidential Directive 59; Homeland Security Presidential Directive 24, (2008). http://www.whitehouse.gov/news/releases/2008/06/20080605-8.html

Privacy Office. (2007). *Privacy Technology Implementation Guide*. Washington, DC: U.S. Department of Homeland Security. http://www.dhs.gov/xlibrary/assets/privacy/privacy_guide_ptig.pdf

Sundberg, H. P., and Sandberg, K. W. (2006). Towards e-government: a survey of problems in organizational processes. *Business Process Management Journal, 12*(2).

Swire, P. F., and Butts, C. Q. (2008). *The ID Divide: Addressing the Challenges of Identification and Authentication in American Society*. Washington, DC: The Center for American Progress. http://www.americanprogress.org/issues/2008/06/pdf/id_divide.pdf

The President's Identity Theft Task Force. (2007). *Combating Identity Theft: A Strategic Plan*. Washington, DC: The Office of the President of the United States. http://www.idtheft.gov/reports/StrategicPlan.pdf

Annex M Acronyms

ABACWG	Attribute Based Access Control Working Group
ANSI	American National Standards Institute
AWG	GSA HSPD-12 architecture working group
CAC	Common Access Card
CDC	Centers for Disease Control and Prevention
CIO	Chief Information Officer
CJIS	Criminal Justice Information Services
CONOPS	Concept of Operations
CPMWG	DOD PKI Certificate Policy Management Working Group
DHS	Department of Homeland Security
DOC	Department of Commerce
DOD	Department of Defense
DOE	Department of Energy
DOJ	Department of Justice
DOS	Department of State
EPTWG	Evaluation Program Technical Working Group
FAA	Federal Aviation Administration

FBCA	Federal Bridge Certificate Authority
FBI	Federal Bureau of Investigation
FEA	Federal Enterprise Architecture
FICC	Federal Identity Credential Committee
FIPS	Federal Information Processing Standard
FISMA	Federal Information Security Management Act
FRAC	First Responder's Access Card
FTC	Federal Trade Commission
GIG	Global Information Grid
GSA	General Services Administration
GTG	Global Telecommunications Grid
HHS	Department of Health and Human Services
HIPAA	Health Insurance Portability and Accountability Act
HR	Human Resources
IA	Information Assurance
ICCP	Committee for Information, Computer and Communications Policy
ICT	Information and Communications Technology
IdM	Identity Management
IdMN	IdM Network

IPMSCG	DOD Identity Protection and Management Senior Co-ordinating Group
IRS	Internal Revenue Service
ISE	Information Sharing Environment
ISO	International Organization for Standardization
ISO/IEC/JTC1/SC27	IT Security Techniques
IT	Information Technology
ITU	International Telecommunication Union
ITU-D	Development Sector
ITU-R	Radiocommunication Sector
ITU-T	Telecommunication Sector
NASA	National Aeronautics and Space Administration
NIH	National Institutes of Health
NIST	National Institute of Standards and Technology
NOAA	National Oceanic and Atmospheric Administration
NSF	National Science Foundation
NSS	National Security System
NSTC	National Science and Technology Committee
OECD	Organization for Economic Cooperation and Development
OMB	Office of Management and Budget

OPM	Office of Personnel Management
PIA	Privacy Impact Assessment
PII	Personally Identifiable Information
PIN	Personal Identification Number
PIV	Personal Identity Verification
PKI	Public Key Infrastructure
PSTN	Public-Switched Telecommunications Network
SCA	SmartCard Alliance
SDO	Standards Development Organization
SG17	ITU-T standards group on security
SIA	Security Industry Alliance (SIA)
SOA	Service Oriented Architecture
SORN	System of Records Notice
SSA	Social Security Administration
SSN	Social Security number
STAR	Staff Time and Activity Reporting
TSP	Thrift Savings Plan
TWIC	Transportation Worker Identification Card
VA	Department of Veterans Affairs
WPISP	Working Party on Information Security and Privacy

Annex N National Science and Technology Council, Committee on Technology

Co-Chair: Richard Russell, Office of Science and Technology Policy
Co-Chair: C.H. Albright, Department of Energy
Co-Chair: James Turner, National Institute of Standards and Technology
Executive Secretary: Jason Boehm, National Institute of Standards and Technology

Membership

Department of Agriculture

Department of Defense
Andre van Tilborg

Department of Commerce
Joel Harris

Department of Energy
Ray Orbach

Department of Education
Tim Magner

Department of Health and Human Services
Charles Johnson

Department of Homeland Security
Robert Hooks

Department of Interior

Department of Justice

James McAtamney

Department of Labor
Brent Orrell

Department of Transportation
Jeff Shane

Department of Treasury
Scott Parsons

National Aeronautics and Space Administration
Shana Dale

National Science Foundation
Kathie Olsen

National Institutes of Health
Mark Rohrbaugh

Central Intelligence Agency
John Phillips

Environmental Protection Agency
George Gray

www.ingramcontent.com/pod-product-compliance
Lightning Source LLC
Chambersburg PA
CBHW081207280526
45787CB00006B/2357